FOSTERING LEADERSHIP EXCELLENCE IN INDIAN BANKS

INSPIRING INSIGHTS FOR MEETING LEADERSHIP CHALLENGES

V.CHANDRASEKHARAN

Made with ♥ on the Notion Press Platform
www.notionpress.com

Dedicated to My Beloved Parents

Invaluable lessons imparted by my parents still resonate deeply with in me, with the one quoted below standing out prominently:

"Even when presented with an abundance of wealth and fame, never forget that the life lessons you learned are more valuable than that."

Dear father and mother, your wisdom continues to guide and inspire me.

Contents

"What we have done for ourselves dies with us, what we have done for others and the world, remains and is immortal."

-Albert Pike

Acknowledgements

At the outset, I would like to express my sincere gratitude to Prof. Biju Varkkey, HRM, Indian Institute of Management (IIM), Ahmedabad, for graciously taking time from his demanding schedule to write the foreword for this book. The professor's scholarly insights and valuable perspective in the foreword have added immense value to the book. I thank him so much for his kindness and generosity.

I am greatly indebted to Sri G. G. Menon, a former Principal of the erstwhile Syndicate Bank's Staff Training College, Ernakulam but for whose unstinted co-operation and meticulousness, taking this project to a successful conclusion would have been really difficult for me. He is unassuming and understated brilliance personified with a special knack for reviewing and editing manuscripts. His voracious reading habit and the stint in a news agency's editorial desk prior to joining the bank enabled him develop these special skills. I salute the enormous patience, diligence and clear conscience with which he went through the manuscript, made value additions and editing to make it direct, crisp and thought-provoking. Besides, Sri. Menon has also kindly allowed me to include in this book his article titled, "The fight against money laundering - an explainer" for the benefit of the readers.

My thanks are due to Sri K.A.Kamath, the first Principal of the erstwhile Syndicate Bank's Staff Training College, Ernakulam who inducted me into the Bank's Training Department as a Faculty Member. My stint as a Faculty Member/Principal in the training system, cumulatively for about 11 years, out of more than 34 years of my total service in the bank, has enabled me enhance academic bent of mind and self-development.

I take this opportunity to express my heartfelt gratitude to Prof. S.Ganesan, a well-known educationist in Tamil Nadu, who occupied various positions, including the Director of several Business Schools in Coimbatore, for offering me unstinted support and patronage for furthering my academic interest during the initial period of my retirement from the bank.

I take this opportunity to thank Sri. P.R.Chandramohanan, Chief Manager(Retired) of Federal Bank, who first introduced me to Personal Counselling, which eventually acted as the impetus for me to successfully complete a course on MS (Counselling).

I thank Sri K. Abdul Ahad, my long-term friend and class-mate at college and a former Chief Manager, Bank of Baroda, for sharing with me his valuable insights on the past, present and emerging leadership scenarios in Indian banks, which has added considerable value to the contents.

My thanks are due to Ms. Anakha Baburaj, Publishing Consultant, Notion Press, for her helpful information, advice and suggestions during the publication process of the book.

I express my sincere gratitude to Ms. Judith Melinda, publishing manager, for completing the interior typesetting and management of the book very nicely and diligently.

I also express my deep gratitude to my wife Veena for her continuous encouragement amid stressful writing process.

Foreword

Though modern banking in India started in the 17th century, informally organized banking activity has existed in this land since much older times. It has found mention even in the Vedas and other ancient texts. Since it made its appearance, modern banking in India has come a long way with multiple inflection points, some of them critical in nature. Today, the country can be proud of its elaborate banking ecosystem which is well in with the global financial system. While it is wide and growing wider, it is also deep and gaining greater depth, supported by its technological prowess. Its impressive network is complemented by physical and digital presence with high touch, high speed and high regulation as distinguishing features.

Multiple challenges are emerging across the world like VUCA (Volatility, Uncertainty, Complexity and Ambiguity), BANI (Brittle, Anxious, Non-linear, Incomprehensible), RUPT (Rapid, Unpredictable, Paradoxical and Tangled) or TUNA (Turbulent, Uncertain, Novel and Ambiguous). A banker's life too is impacted by changes happening elsewhere, be it in one's own country or abroad. Meeting these challenges requires a well-grounded understanding of the fundamental principles and a flexible mindset to embrace the new realities.

The book "Fostering Leadership Excellence in Indian Banks – Inspiring insights for meeting leadership challenges" by the experienced banker, V Chandrasekharan is primarily intended for use by mid-level and junior officers who are already performing a leadership role and who want to excel in that role as well as the new entrants who aspire to occupy leadership roles in future. At the same time, the book can equally well serve as a contextual resource book on leadership for all bankers, from the top leadership downwards. A distinct feature of this book is the combination of relevant theory on leadership and banking with the deep insights gained by the author from the trenches i.e. the challenging world of commercial banking in India.

The first chapter of the book starts with a very simple yet profound and insightful quote about excellence from John W Gardner, "Excellence is doing ordinary things extraordinarily well" and goes on to connect it to leadership. Growing and becoming a leader is a journey in itself, and at many points, individuals do ask questions of clarificatory nature about the qualities of a leader and the parameters of leadership excellence. While numerous books and scholarly writings on leadership excellence exist, distilling the wealth of knowledge, wisdom and insights in them into a cohesive book has always posed a challenge. Mr. Chandrasekharan, however, has successfully managed to do this in his book. He has identified eighteen distinct qualities as essential for a successful leader (may not be exhaustive and complete) starting with integrity, with a simple explanation about why it is important with illustrations taken from everyday life of a banker. It's a good start for the many good things to come later in the book.

The book also deals with many factors that are critical to a banker's life, the organization and the national economy. The most challenging task for a commercial banker is dealing with credit proposals, taking credit decisions and managing the associated risks. Chapter 4 - dealing with credit and how to be a good credit officer and the competencies required to be learned to demonstrate leadership in credit - contains useful and in-depth discussions on these important aspects of credit management. Like many seasoned bankers, I too believe that credit is the lifeline of a banking system, involving as it does, significant amount of decision-making, use of data and application of mind. To be a successful banking leader, an officer must understand how the credit process works and know how to balance the internal and external factors that have a bearing on a credit decision. No doubt, credit decision-making has its vulnerabilities but the way out is not to stop lending or becoming risk-averse which can affect the business adversely. Instead, it must be ensured that due diligence, care and caution is never compromised in matters related to credit. A banker needs to be a trusted advisor/ counselor to the customer and in that capacity, he must show the required professionalism with a human touch. Even in these days of algorithm-based lending, digital banking and contactless banking, having a human touch and building trust of customers are critical to success.

Readers of the book will be taken on an exciting journey through the different dimensions of leadership excellence like how to communicate, importance of knowledge management and customer service. In the chapter on Knowledge Management, readers will find short explanations (snapshots) of key terms frequently used by bankers in day-to-day conversations and during the decision-making process. These snapshots should help one have the conceptual clarity required while handling important matters.

Knowing and managing oneself help the incumbent to deal with decision situations and dilemmas, confidently and calmly. It also helps him to balance compliance and customer experience, to maintain positive team environment and to build a sustainable organization that balances the quadruple result requirements of people, planet, profit and purpose. While a bank's HR Department, the executives and the immediate supervisor can support the individual leader in the leadership journey, the individual's own sense of responsibility and commitment are of paramount importance. It may not be out of place to mention here that lack of focus on the softer side of leadership has often been found to be the prime reason for leadership failure and burnout with high cost to the individual and the organization. The book has addressed this aspect adequately.

Success of a leader also depends on the ability to manage multiple constituencies - primarily, the customer who is the reason for the organization's existence and the branch as the unit to connect to the customer - along with a good macro-level understanding of the organization (bank) in terms of structure, strategy and deliverables i.e. profitability in the right way and the people management or HRM, including structure and culture building. The chapter on branch management deals with how branch-based leadership can be developed. The insights in the book should serve as guideposts to the aspiring leaders as they prepare to evolve as effective leaders. To prepare for the journey they need support in matters like training, mentoring, coaching, counseling, developing leader impact supporting attitudes and gathering varied experiences. While the organization has to institutionalize suitable and agile organizational structures and enabling HR polices for training and performance evaluation, the importance of the role an individual should play cannot be under-emphasized.

Finally, the proof of the pudding is in eating it. The case study of the transformation effected in South Indian Bank by its MD and CEO, Dr. V.A.Joseph through effective application of leadership principles should inspire all bankers. From the learning perspective, case studies are excellent examples for others to learn from and also, to understand how organizational processes are executed. The concluding words of Dr Joseph, re-emphasizing the need to balance the predictable and the unpredictable together, without losing sight of the organization's purpose, incidentally summarize the very essence of the book. Effective leaders are the outcome of a long journey, and they create positive impact on people, build performing teams, ensure organizational sustainability and still remain humane and humble. Before concluding, let me say this: I cannot agree more not just with the moral of the SIB story, but also with the author's discourse on spreading the culture of leadership excellence in Indian banking.

Prof. Biju Varkkey
Human Resource Management Area
Indian Institute of Management, Ahmedabad

Author's Note

"Nothing else in the world... not all the armies...is so powerful as an idea whose time has come."
-Victor Hugo.

It is a great paradox of our times that even as our lives have become many times better than the lives lived by the past generations of men and women in terms of resources, comforts, safety and security, the quality of our lives in many other respects has simultaneously witnessed a steep decline over the last few decades. From the air we breathe in to the quality of education imparted in government schools, there is hardly any area today which does not give you cause for concern. Any serious and objective enquiry into the causes behind this sorry state of affairs will tell us that a major reason is the weakening influence in society of the timeless value systems based on principled conduct passed down to us by our forebears and our scriptures. As a result, today, the very attitudes, approaches and behaviours which were frowned upon till a few decades ago are not only accepted but also appreciated by many. I am referring to things like unethical conduct, the killer instinct, the profit-at-any-cost approach, the lack of scruples and the utter disregard for public interest.

Clearly, the most effective way of resolving many of our problems is instilling high ethical standards in human beings from the beginning and encouraging and supporting them to stay the course throughout their lives. Stephen R Covey has rightly said, ***"Peace of mind comes when your life is in harmony with true principles and values and in no other way."*** I fully agree with Mr. Covey. In fact, throughout my life, both officially as a bank officer and privately as a responsible citizen, I have always assiduously tried to impress upon everyone who cared to listen, the importance of ethics, honesty, integrity and probity in life. In fact, it is this abiding commitment to promote these virtues in public life, especially at the higher echelons, that prompted me to write this book. Naturally, the aforesaid commitment is the defining feature of the book and it runs like a common thread through its various chapters.

Many people mistakenly believe that if you strictly adhere to ethics, you are not likely to succeed in business. It is only proper that I address this issue here. The above belief is normally held only by those who shun hard work and want to get everything easily on a platter. But, this approach can never guarantee success. Besides, short-cuts could also land one in all kinds of trouble. In fact, ethical behaviour helps one's business to enjoy continued success for as long as one wants by reaping the following benefits. To mention just a few of them, ethical behaviour gets you the trust of your stakeholders and your customers; your brands gain the trust and love of the customers as exemplified by the Tata brands; your adherence to ethics enhances your reputation; being ethical reduces the possibility of rash decisions thus helping risk mitigation; working for a business which follows ethical practices improve employee morale and enhances their sense of belonging. Given the above, I have no hesitation in saying that regardless of who we are and what we do to earn a living, *being truly ethical in our thoughts, speech and actions is an idea whose time has come.*

"One man cannot do right in one department of life whilst he is occupied in doing wrong in any other department. Life is one indivisible whole."
-Gandhiji

Introduction

Indian banking post-nationalisation - An overview

During the post-nationalization decades, the banking scene in India has undergone a sea change. First and foremost, this period saw remarkable widening and deepening of the banking sector. At the time of nationalization of 14 major banks in 1969, the total number of bank branches stood at 8,261. In 2023, the number had swelled to over 1.62 lakhs branches and ATMs over 2.66 lakhs. The number of unbanked centres in the country has been considerably brought down thanks to the liberalization of the Branch Authorization Policy of RBI and licensing of many new private banks and small finance banks. And where opening a branch in a place is difficult, banks have been trying to make up for it by appointing banking correspondents to carry out certain primary banking functions on their behalf.

The widening reach of banks has also been accompanied by a shift from 'class banking' to 'mass banking'. Today, banks cater to the saving and credit needs of various sections of the society, offering a range of sophisticated deposits and loan products. It may be mentioned here that the phenomenal progress witnessed by various sectors of the economy viz. agriculture, dairying, MSMEs, transporters etc post-1969, would not have been possible without the support of priority sector credit of banks across the country.

The extraordinary growth of the banking sector also increased the exposure of banks to various kinds of risks, which in turn resulted in ensuring foolproof risk management systems and capital adequacy of banks. As a result, the country adopted the Basel norms for capital adequacy in the 1990s. In line with these norms, the methodology and practices relating to oversight and inspection of banks by RBI and of individual bank branches by their controlling offices have also been suitably modified and refined.

The massive increase in bank branches also led to the spread of banking habit among more and more people and manifold growth in banking transactions. This has necessitated recruitment of clerical hands and officers on an unprecedented scale over a period of about two decades, starting in the early 1970s. Towards the end of the 1990s, the operational challenges posed by the phenomenal increase in the volume of banking transactions gave a strong push to computerization in banks. By the turn of the century, all banks, from the biggest to the smallest, have fully computerized their operations. The consequential staff redundancy was addressed by banks through attractive voluntary retirement schemes.

In recent times, the critical challenges of surging NPAs and maintaining capital adequacy have been posing existential threat to many banks. This has led to acquisitions and mega-mergers of public sector banks. After three rounds of consolidation, the number of PSBs has shrunk from 27 in March 2017 to 12 in April 2020. As a part of this process, 10 smaller PSBs were merged with 5 major PSBs, namely Punjab National Bank, Bank of Baroda, Canara Bank, Union Bank of India and Indian Bank. Post-merger, the five banks have been able to achieve substantial economies of scale and their earning capacity too has increased to a considerable extent.

The digital paradigm has fundamentally changed every banking activity and presented three major challenges before the banks to cope with, namely, making and adapting to major changes in the traditional work style, getting used to the profit-at-any-cost approach to business and unprecedented increase in work-related stress faced by employees. Out of the three challenges, the first and the third one directly impact the human resources at the banks' disposal.

As the sophisticated digital technology has brought down the curtain on the longstanding manual operations there emerges a realization that digital technology *per se* is not sufficient to ensure the success of a bank. The workforce must be adequately equipped to use the latest technological tools and also ensure that they must possess the capacity and skills to navigate the numerous challenges thrown up almost on a daily basis in areas as diverse as marketing of products, public relations, deposit mobilization, credit management, risk management, recovery management, motivation and management of staff, to name just a few.

In a nutshell, leveraging technology needs to be complemented by capacity-building and motivation of staff for the success of a bank. While identifying the true potential of an employee, efforts must be made to transform even an ordinary employee into an extraordinary performer. Those holding managerial positions across an organization, whether in charge of line functions or staff functions are supposed to have robust leadership qualities in them. The book specifically aims at creating profound awareness on leadership and standards of excellence among the officers and staff in the bottom level of the pyramid, as they are the real wealth creators. Let me hasten to add that every officer or staff member need not be made or designated as a de jure leader, but strengthening of leadership orientation to the branch level officers and staff can enable them share, care, lead and live better and make them more responsible. As the leadership qualities mentioned here are of fundamentally virtuous in nature, an employee at any level can be enlightened to discover the 'leader' in him/her through educational and transformative initiatives. Those who already play the role of a leader in a bank will find this book helpful to influence and inspire their colleagues. As Goethe remarked, "Treat a man as he is and you can make him worse than he is; treat a man as he has the potential to become and you make him better than he is."

Chapter 1, Leadership in Banks – Achieving Excellence, focuses on the building blocks of leadership excellence. It discusses at length a template of 18 essential qualities such as Integrity, Vision, Communication, Empathy, Humility, Delegation etc required for leadership excellence. These are certain qualities without which a leader is going to find himself seriously handicapped while dealing with the various challenges of his job. Most of these qualities are part of the ancient Indian wisdom which can be used as a credible guide to revitalise contemporary leadership behaviour in banks. Chapter 2, Leadership in banks – Today and Tomorrow, discusses leadership in action in the present and what it holds in future. The author observes that many bankers who exercise leadership in Indian banks assume it as a function of position. Chapter 3 deals with Re-imagining organizational structure of banks.

Chapter 4 to 10, spotlight on seven indispensable leadership skills for bankers, which help them develop their capacity building roles. The skills like credit management, knowledge management, communication, time management, maintaining good health and managing stress etc serve as tools to broaden their knowledge, skill and attitude and enhance their overall performance in a big way.

Chapters from 11 to 15 deal with issues such as Profit Maximisation: the right way, Branch Manager: the woes and opportunities, Work-life-balance of the staff etc which are extremely challenging for many of the staff members. Money laundering is highly engaging subject in recent years as it has become a bane in the financial world. Today, money laundering threatens peace, stability and prosperity in many societies across the globe. Hence, every banker should know the intricacies of the money laundering process before handling them effectively.

Chapter 16, titled 'The Transformational Saga of South Indian Bank', is a fascinating case study of one of the most talked-about turnarounds ever in the history of Indian banking. In fact, this case study most effectively conveys the central message of this book that by using these leadership qualities in a well-planned, skilful and synergised way, a true leader can not only steer an organization out of trouble but also take it to unprecedented levels of growth and development from where there is no looking back.

It was my good fortune to work in various branches of Syndicate Bank (a leading public sector bank till it was merged with Canara Bank) both as officer and senior branch manager. During my nearly three and a half decades of service, I also worked as a faculty member/Head of the bank's two training colleges for about 11 years and as recovery officer and inspecting officer in the bank's regional offices. My experiences through different roles, postings and designations have reinforced my belief that without leadership excellence at all levels, any bank may find it difficult to realize its full potential. This book is based on the insights that I could gather through my experiences in the bank and interactions with the executives and staff of various banks, cutting across hierarchies.

Banks are service oriented organizations and every service moment touches the lives of the customers. The model I have envisaged in the book is a win-win proposition for the workforce and all other stakeholders of banks. The unique feature of the book is that it is easy to read and conversational. As you read this repeatedly, you will discover that it is a continual source of blossoming your creativity. If the talents of the highly resourceful workforce are put to use the best way possible, the work culture of the young branch managers and officers of both the public sector and private sector banks in India will undergo a remarkable change. The whole idea is not to prepare them to become MDs or CEOs or Executive Directors, but to equip them with the skills to excel in their work, while also enable them enjoy satisfying lives as members of the society at large.

No work can claim to be the final word on a subject notwithstanding all the research and hard work that might have preceded its production. Therefore, constructive suggestions from discerning readers for improving the quality of this book are always welcome.

V.Chandrasekharan

CHAPTER 1

Leadership In Banks - Achieving Excellence

"The quality of a person's life is in direct proportion of his commitment to excellence."
- Vincent Lombardi

"Excellence is doing ordinary things extraordinarily well."
-John W Gardner

It is always good to be clear about what leadership means before commencing a discussion on the topic. Therefore, let us start with the definition of 'Leadership'. There are many definitions of leadership and the one which comes closest to being a simple yet complete definition of leadership is what P.G.Northouse has said, "Leadership is a process whereby an individual influences a group of individuals to achieve a common goal."

The need for leadership could arise in a variety of human activities performed in groups e.g. business, education, politics and social work. Better the quality of leadership available, the better will be the performance of the group and hence, the better the prospects of achieving the goals before the group. It should be noted that leadership is not the same as management. A manager essentially exercises his authority and control to ensure that day-to-day operations of an organization are performed, as expected. A leader, on the other hand influences, motivates and enables the team members to give their best towards achieving the organizational goals. It must be noted that management and leadership are not mutually exclusive, you can have them both.

Leadership is not a mysterious phenomenon seen only among the top executives or statesmen or politicians of larger-than-life stature. In fact, leadership qualities lie latent in all, but it is clearly noticeable only in a few. Such individuals who are not aware of the leader in them, would need some grooming and mentoring before they shed their diffidence.

What makes a leader different from others is that he has a plan and a vision, along with the ability to influence others, to work towards achieving the set objectives.

History is replete with many outstanding examples of how even ordinary people were able to transfer themselves into extraordinary leaders. The ambitious journey of the great Abraham Lincoln, former U.S. President from a log cabin to the White House has been the stuff of legends and continues to inspire humanity. The transformation of Mohandas Karamchand Gandhi from a shy child to the leader of a mass freedom movement continues to be an enduring testimony of what the human spirits can achieve. The journey of our present Prime Minister Narendra Modi, from a tea seller to the Prime Minister of the largest democracy in the world, by dint of his hard work and dedication is no less inspiring.

What is Leadership Excellence

Achieving excellence means surpassing the existing standards of performance or be the best at something. As Ralf Marston says, "Excellence is not a skill, it is an attitude". All leaders and aspiring leaders will do well to recognise the following realities if they are aiming at leadership excellence. First, recognizing the reality of dependency relationships is a *sine qua non* for being a successful leader. Secondly, in order to develop the hidden competencies of individuals and use them for the development of the organization, promoting and nurturing a co-ordinated, collaborative and creative approach in all areas is essential. Thirdly, a leader should continually inspire and develop himself so that his personal example spreads a culture of excellence across the organization. It is relevant to recall the words of Aristotle here: “We are what we repeatedly do. Excellence then is not an act, but a habit.”

The best way to understand what leadership excellence is to understand what they are not. For instance, let’s take ten positive qualities; negative leadership qualities are shown in the brackets.

1. Integrity (Acting without integrity) 2. Resilience (Absence of resilience) 3. Good communication (Poor communication) 4. Empathy (Lack of empathy) 5. Good learning (Poor learning) 6. Good Delegation

(Poor delegation) 7. Humility (Arrogance) 8. Good decision-making (Poor decision-making) 9. Creative (No innovation) 10. Responsible (Irresponsible)

Think about a hypothetical situation where many bank officers follow the negative qualities mentioned above; sooner or later the bank will fail. We know that the employees of some low performing banks have the same level of education, age, experience as compared to the workforce of the high performing banks. It is in this context one must think about the relevance of leadership excellence.

Efficiency and effectiveness:To make leadership excellence further clear, we have to distinguish it with efficiency and the effectiveness. Efficiency is the quality of doing something well without wastage of resources like time, money etc or to put it simply, efficiency aims at *doing things right*. Effectiveness, on the other hand, means *seeking and doing the right things.* In fact, these two qualities are complementary to each other. A team that gives priority to effectiveness over efficiency may spend too much time and resources on the task involved which in terms of cost may far outweigh the gains expected from the project. As both are important for the success of a team, the leader should not only identify that it is done well by the team (Efficiency) but also ensure the right thing to do (Effectiveness). Briefly put, a team leader should aim at being efficiently effective. As Peter Drucker said, “Management is doing things right; leadership is doing the right things.”

Essential qualities for leadership excellence

We now discuss below the qualities essential for achieving ‘Leadership excellence’ with special reference to Indian banks.

1. Integrity

As C.S. Lewis once said, "Integrity is doing the right thing even when no one is watching." It is the most desirable quality in a banker as his job requires him to be the trustee of other people’s money. He must always be ethically strong and morally transparent in his dealings with the customers and other stakeholders. How can people believe or trust a dishonest leader? Unfortunately, like in any other domain, banking industry too has its share of tainted leaders. Leaders should not only be principled and morally upright but also appear to be so. This means that their conduct and dealings must be totally transparent.

2. *Vision*

Vision is the ability to see what lies far ahead. It is imagining the target. A leader, who is a visionary, thinks with a long-term perspective. His vision is like a compelling dream to be communicated clearly and translated into reality. Bill Gates of Microsoft had a clear vision of a personal computer on every desk in America when he ventured out on his business journey. Steve Jobs' vision for Apple was "Building tools that amplify human ability". It is noteworthy that he used the words "tools" and not "computers" and that is why Apple could make not just iPad but also iPod, iPhone and iTunes which revolutionised how people listened to music. Both Bill Gates and Steve Job were university drop-outs. But, they were outstanding talents in their own fields who could always focus on the big picture in their minds' eye and work towards its realisation. Their discoveries have today radically changed the lifestyle of people around the world.

3. *Resilience*

Resilience is the ability to bounce back from adversity or hardships. Resilient leaders recover more quickly from a crisis and learn from disruptions like Covid-19 lockdown situations. They are unruffled to combat the crisis and will keep the team positive. They can influence and inspire the team members to be aware of their power, wisdom and creativity and keep going towards their destination, no matter how impossible the journey is. The leaders of banks have to imbibe resilience so that the stakeholders can feel safe and remain confident and motivated.

4. *Responsibility*

Responsibility and self-discipline help leaders achieve their dreams and goals. A leader may have the capacity to scale great heights in his profession, but without self-discipline and responsibility, he cannot remain there for long. Good leaders are proactive and never reactive. They are always keen to update their knowledge and skills. They not only work hard, but work smart too. They are decisive and driven by excellence.

5.Communication

The best leaders communicate with team members candidly, objectively and effectively to achieve the organisational goals. The fundamental aim of communication is to create mutual understanding. The components of communication are reading, writing, speaking and listening. Bankers shall be good listeners. Peter Drucker believed that 60% of all management problems are the results of faulty communication and poor listening. Attentive listening helps to understand others' perspectives accurately; it also helps in enhancing trust and mutual respect between a leader and the team members. Clarity and simplicity make communication effective. In order to be a good communicator, a leader should be resourceful, ready-witted and be aware of what is happening around him.

6. Relationships

A leader should be sensitive to the needs of the people and must display caring and loving attitude toward them. Caring leaders make their own lives, as well as lives of other people comfortable. As has been rightly said, the more we give, the more we get back. "Treat others as you would want them to treat you", is the universal Golden rule. *Mahabharata* (XVIII – 113.8) says, "One should never do to another what one regards as injurious to oneself. This in brief is the law of *Dharma*." Needless to say, this is one of the most important qualities required for a leader.

7. Humility

Humility is critical to effective leadership, yet it is conspicuously absent in many leaders due to 'Ego affliction'. This malady can take different forms e.g. a leader spending more time on self-promotion than doing something constructive; a leader ignoring or poking holes when ideas or suggestions are put forward by others; a leader ridiculing those who are more knowledgeable or smarter than him; a leader refusing to accept that his decision was wrong. One cannot gain mastery over all areas of knowledge nor have answers to all questions at any point of time. On such occasions, it is better to seek the advice of those who know better. Otherwise, one is not only sabotaging one's own growth but also sabotaging the performance and growth of the entire team. This aspect has added relevance in today's world where it is not surprising to see a junior officer or a clerk whose academic credentials are more impressive than that of his superiors.

8. Empathy

Empathy simply is the ability to understand deeply the experience of another person along with the capacity to imagine oneself in the situation of that person and experiencing the emotions, ideas and perspectives of that person. Empathetic listening can change the quality of interpersonal relationship in the family and workplace. Empathetic leaders can create a feeling of warmth and trust in the workplace which could drive the employees to be more hardworking and productive. This facilitates the emergence of a win-win situation for both, the organization and its workforce.

9. Credibility

This is the quality that makes leaders believable and trustworthy. A credible leader always walks the talk and practises what he preaches. When the team is traversing uncharted territory or facing new dangers, he leads by example and acts as a good role model for others. He does not bad-mouth people who are not present. He is dead against rumour-mongering. He never fails to acknowledge and praise the worthy contributions of his team members.

10. Forgiveness

We live in an imperfect world and that people make mistakes. Forgiveness makes life simple and pleasant. Forgiveness is not an act of surrendering to another. We need not change the other person or agree with him, but by forgiving we can ensure peace within ourselves. To forgive is a goal towards happiness, not to forgive is a decision to suffer. Winning the battle inside the mind is the greatest victory than winning hundreds of battles outside. Therefore, free yourself from negative energy; forgive and move on. Remember, forgiveness and patience must go hand in hand.

11. Sense of humour

Humour is skill which can be trained and learned easily. It helps the leader to know their employees more intimately and in turn, enhance personal likeability to connect him closely. Gentle humour helps to narrow down the positional difference, defuse stressful situations in work, minimise health problems and improve productivity. At best, it can generate a sense of freedom and stimulate innovation.

12. Continuous learning

Often an executive who has reached a high position in his organization has the tendency to think that he knows enough about a subject and therefore, he has nothing more to learn. Such a line of thinking is most erroneous and can hinder one's mental and psychological development. Learning is a never-ending process. A leader must continually assess his/her strength and weaknesses. When such exercise indicates areas of weaknesses, he should try to learn or unlearn or relearn, as the case may be, to overcome the weaknesses. Otherwise, it will be difficult for him to meet the challenges of today's dynamic world. It may be mentioned here that many of the well-known leaders the world over, are known to be great learners.

13. Delegation

Delegation is an important management skill. It means transferring the responsibility of performing one or more tasks from oneself to another person. When you delegate a task, you are not only facilitating teamwork, but also empowering your team members by making them autonomous to make decisions. Some leaders may avoid delegation for a variety of reasons e.g. the fear that it may take much longer to explain things to another person than doing it himself/herself, the fear that delegation may reduce the indispensability of the leader to the team; lack of confidence in the person to whom a task is to be delegated. The leader's trust in the team members and his own trustworthiness are decisive factors for the success of delegation. Delegation helps to develop the initiative, judgement and other talents of team members and improves the collective performance of the team.

14. Decision making capabilities

A leader must have the ability to correctly define the problems, identify and examine the possible solutions, select the best one among them and go ahead with the execution. While taking decisions, he should neither be too hasty nor be a procrastinator. And once he takes a decision, he should have the confidence to stick to it and make a success of it.

15. Creativity and innovativeness

A leader needs to act as a thought leader to the team and encourage creativity and out-of-the-box thinking among team members. In today's world, change is the only thing that does not change; everything else is subject to change. Given this, banks always sticking to the beaten track are likely to find it difficult to survive. Executives and officers in leadership roles should not remain satisfied with staff members doing things right only. They must also ignite the latent creativity and innovativeness within them and encourage them to use their talents to find ways to do things better, faster and more economically.

16. Courage

Courage is a quality much needed by leaders which enables them to move ahead in the proper direction. Courage is what makes you face an imminent danger head on. Courageous leaders realize that in the midst of turbulence, there lies an extraordinary opportunity to grow and rise. A good leader is never afraid to ask questions or put forth a new idea even to his superiors for he knows that avoidance behaviour may lead to problems or conflicts later on. Good leaders welcome honest feedback and will never blame the team for failures or shortcomings. They come forward to own up full responsibility and always make their team feel that they are supportive and stand solidly behind them as long as they are fighting for a just and right cause. At the same time, they sternly deal with those who are lax in discharging their responsibilities or whose actions run counter to team spirit which is essential for the success of the team.

17. Motivational skills

In every group, there will be people with attitudinal problems and/or less than the desired level of commitment to work. A leader should be able to inspire everyone in his team to give his/her best to the organization, irrespective of the kind of job he or she is doing. For example, a sweeper or an attender or a clerk must never be made to feel that the jobs they are doing are anyway inferior to the jobs of their superiors. Instead, they should be motivated to take ownership of their job and feel proud of it.

18. Emotional intelligence

This is the ability to perceive, understand, interpret, demonstrate, control and manage your own emotions and those of other people around you. People with a high EI quotient know what emotions they are feeling, what these emotions mean and how they affect their own behaviour and that of others. This ability helps one to stay calm under pressure and think rationally before reacting. Emotional intelligence is very essential for good interpersonal relationship and improved well-being of oneself and others. Daniel Goleman suggests that along with technical and intellectual skills, the corporate leaders must possess traits and competencies covered by the term emotional intelligence like self-awareness, self-regulation, motivation, empathy, social skills etc.

These qualities, however, are not comprehensive, anyway. There are still many more qualities which are not hard to identify and that there is nothing intimidating about acquiring these qualities. These finest leadership qualities mentioned above are not new, and many of which are integral part of Indian ethos and have been with us for several millennia. Most of these qualities are closely aligned to the nature's principles and time-tested values. The banks can initiate leadership education and awareness among the officers and staff as part of putting into place the vision of 'new generational leadership' in the journey ahead. This is an empowering 'leadership from below' approach. An effective training can awaken them and go a long way to strengthen their will. For example, let's take the indispensable leadership quality of resilience. Every human acquires this quality soon after birth. A human baby has to pass through different stages to reach the stage of walking. When he reaches that stage, he has to struggle for many days to stand on his legs and get the balance right. Despite the falls, pains and tears, the baby doesn't give up and bounces back after each failure. This quality stays with most of us till the end. Given the necessary will and dedication, there is nothing that human beings cannot learn. As the idiom goes, 'where there is a will, there is a way'.

The technological revolution brings fantastic and frightening change but these timeless qualities should never be allowed to undergo any change. The bankers should embrace them as standard operating qualities in their daily life and work. The superiors may give a feeling of importance to the staff in their respective ecosystems. If all the executives and officers practise these positive leadership qualities sincerely and in obedience to moral and ethical order, the much-aspired sustainable development of the organisations will be a certainty. As Primo Levi rightly said, "Things whose existence is not morally comprehensible cannot exist". When right attitude is stabilized as a culture in their mind, their greatest calling in the planet earth will be fructified. Eventually they will think beyond the warped incentives and display dedication as their way of life.*(Please also read Author's Note and Annexure II ("Leadership Excellence -The Taj way").*

The seasoned executives can act as their mentors to transform them into well-balanced personalities with the necessary skills to do full justice to their leadership roles. Warren G. Bennis, a pioneer in leadership studies has aptly stated: ***"The most dangerous leadership myth is that leaders are born - that there is a genetic factor to leadership. This myth asserts that people simply either have certain charismatic qualities or not. That's nonsense; in fact, the opposite is true. Leaders are made rather than born."***

CHAPTER 2

Leadership In Banks - Today And Tomorrow

"No one is exercising leadership (initiative and influence) because everyone assumes leadership is a function of position."
-Stephen Covey, in his book 'The 8th Habit'

Types of leadership styles

While dealing with the subject of leadership excellence, we should not lose the sight of the critical reference point of management/leadership styles currently in vogue in modern organisations. Therefore, at the outset, it would be in the fitness of things to discuss the four different styles of leadership briefly and also examine which one suits the Indian banks best.

1. Autocratic or Authoritarian style

An authoritarian leadership style is based on authority and control. The leader thinks that he knows what to do and how to control his subordinates. He gives orders and assigns duties and responsibilities without consulting the subordinates. He neither cares for the opinions of the subordinates nor permits them to influence his decisions. This kind of leadership is based upon close supervision, clear-cut direction and the command exercised by the leader. While this kind of style is likely to facilitate quick decisions, prompt actions and unity of direction, too much of it can lead to industrial disputes and strikes. It can also breed frustration among the subordinates as it blocks their creativity. As a result, the subordinates will normally restrict their contribution to the minimum required to escape punishment. Needless to add, this kind of situation is never good for an organization in the long run.

2. The Democratic or Participative Leadership

This type of leader believes in consultation with the subordinates in the formulation of plans and policies. He encourages participation of the subordinates in the decision-making process. He leads by example and uses persuasion rather than taking the help of negative influences like fear, force and punishment to get things done by the subordinates. Here, the leadership is interested in the subordinates, and values their ideas and suggestions. This leads to: (i) higher motivation and improved morale, (ii) increased co-operation with the management, (iii) improved job performance, (iv) reduction of absenteeism and employee turnover.

3. The Laissez-Faire Leadership

Under this management style, the leader passes on the responsibility for decision-making to his subordinates and keeps his role in administration to the minimum. He allows his subordinates a great deal of freedom, sometimes beyond what is good for the organization. He believes that the subordinates will put forth their best efforts if left to themselves and this way the organization can reap maximum benefit. But the experience suggests that in the absence of any direction or control from the side of the leader, most organizations start floundering.

4. Paternalistic leadership

Under this style, the relationship between the leader and the subordinates is like the one between a father (or whoever else is the head of the family) and other members of the family. The leader guides and protects the subordinates and ensures to provide good working conditions, fringe benefits and incentives. The assumption here is that the subordinates will feel grateful and they will work to their fullest capacity for the achievement of the organizational goals. However, it is doubtful if such leadership would be a success with matured and well-educated employees, who may not feel grateful to anyone for salary and incentives received by dint of their hard work.

The Leadership style suits Indian banks best

In fact, there is no style of leadership which is all time best. The best leadership style at a given time will depend on a combination of various factors like the political and socio-economic conditions, the cultural milieu, the nature of the industry, the educational level of the subordinates etc. All things considered, the Democratic or Participative style with its accent on a participative and consultative approach looks most suited to our banks. This style will ensure that the voices and views of the subordinates are heard and recognized. It ensures greater and more active participation in work by all, leading to sustainable and long-lasting improvement in productivity and profitability of the banks.

Dearth of effective leadership – a general phenomenon

Mr. O.P. Bhat, a very successful and celebrated former Chairman of State Bank of India has the following to say about the dearth of effective leadership in our country: “In India there is huge leadership deficit across all classes, whether it is political classes, bankers, bureaucrats, businessmen, social leaders, social thinkers...... often you scratch the top, there is nothing much. For some reason we have stopped producing leaders. There is no insight into the DNA of India unless wise leadership is put across the multiple spectrums." Mr. Bhat said this in 2010, but the situation has not changed much since then. And this has happened in a country of 1.40 billion which not too long ago had an abundance of leaders in almost every walk of life! But, to be fair, this situation is not unique to India. More or less, the same situation prevails in other countries too. Interestingly, this dearth of leadership has coincided with the increasing tendency to globalize and make more and more use of digital technology. Whether it is a mere coincidence or otherwise is not known. Only a detailed study can throw more light on the causal connection, if any, between the factors mentioned above. But, that aspect need not detain us for the time being. Let us now examine some of the factors which have led to the current leadership deficit.

Induction training - filling the gaps

Even as we celebrate 75 years of independence, our outmoded education system remains insensitive to the need for developing leadership qualities among the children. For any job aspirant, getting a job which matches one’s education and skill-set is mostly ruled out in the current scenario for reasons beyond one’s control. The young bank managers and officers in our banks might have passionately chosen diverse disciplines of studies at the under-graduation and post-graduation stages, such as science, arts, management, commerce, engineering, computer science etc with great expectations of entering into a career matching their qualifications and fields of study. For many of them, becoming a bank officer was never a matter of choice, but a compulsive decision for understandable reasons. Needless to say, in a country with a huge unemployment problem, it cannot be otherwise.

After being appointed as probationary officers, these young men and women are normally given two weeks' induction training (theory) at the respective bank's training college at the conclusion of which they are posted to branches for on-the-job training. At the branches, the on-the-job training is rarely systematic as the general tendency is to use the services of probationary officers for clearance of pending work and other issues of concern to the branch management. The problem is accentuated by the fact that today in most banks the number of senior and experienced staff is fast declining due to retirements. This impacts adversely the quality of the on-the-job training, and hand-holding the young probationary officers is indispensable in order to assume leadership positions.

This paradoxical situation tends to nurture the kind of leadership which is based on position and authority. And this is hardly the leadership that banks in India need today. Banks need to try out effective alternative solutions to address the issue. For instance, there could be an arrangement whereby probationary officers could on specified days visit branches headed by performing branch managers and see them in action from close quarters apart from interacting with them on various facets of leadership.

Out-of-the-box leadership approach

Creativity is the defining paradigm of every high performing organization today. In such a scenario, organizations should never be bereft of fresh ideas and this is possible only if there is a never-ending quest for the institutional dynamism. The radical changes brought about by the government through mergers, acquisitions and privatization of banks will be meaningful only if the banks experiment and apply innovative leadership approaches to meet the challenges of the fast-changing scenario.

There is a mistaken notion among many bank staff that leadership is a role played by the top management only. In keeping with this faulty notion, those lower down in the hierarchy seem to believe that their job is just to do the work assigned to them and leave home at the end of the day. This short-sighted approach stands in the way of the inner growth of the employees, which in turn affects the overall development of the organization. At a time when improving capital, maximizing business, enhancing profit, recovering NPAs and mitigating delinquencies in loan accounts have become topmost priorities, the bank employees are expected to contribute much more towards fulfilment of the organizational mission. Needless to say, it is for the managements to come up with innovative solutions to address this issue.

Give public sector banks and their employees the credit they deserve

Currently, many banks are facing existential threats because of increasing NPAs and inadequacy of capital. The government has initiated big-ticket reforms which include mergers, privatization of public sector banks, disinvestment of government shareholding in PSBs, asset monetization etc. While these measures have their merits, the other side of the coin cannot be overlooked. And that other side includes the risk of private owners siphoning off the hard-earned money of the depositors to enrich themselves. The recent cases of alleged siphoning of bank funds by the CEOs of some frontline banks clearly show that such a situation is always a possibility in private banks.

A dispassionate assessment would reveal that the contribution of public sector banks to the sustained growth and development of the banking system in India has not received the recognition it deserves for various reasons. Having been, for about 35 years, a part of Syndicate Bank, a pioneer in many development-oriented banking schemes and projects across the country, I can confidently say that PSBs are one of the very few institutions which can touch the lives of ordinary people in a meaningful and lasting way. This is because of the fact that most of these banks, apart from their customary preoccupation with profit-making, still uphold high principles like commitment to national goals and priorities, concern for the development of the poorest and the weakest, customer service without reservations, high integrity, total transparency etc. while carrying out their operations.

The public sector banks have over the years produced many exemplary leaders. O.P.Bhat, Arundhati Bhattacharya, K.V.Krishnamoorthy and Ranjana Kumar are some of the names that readily come to mind. It is only in recent years that one has been witnessing increasing dearth of effective leadership in the industry. Perhaps, the emergence in recent years of a new ecosystem, characterized by a widespread tendency to rundown public sector banks and their contributions to the development of the nation, has also contributed to the current scenario. This is most unfortunate considering that the building blocks of this country's development were provided chiefly by the public sector.

Removing road-blocks to timely promotions

An average bank employee enters his career with great expectations about climbing the ladder of hierarchy in due course. But, if there are unreasonably long gaps in recruitment to various grades, it can frustrate their career expectations. Let me elaborate. From 1975 to 1985, the banking industry witnessed massive direct recruitment of well-educated youth to various cadres. This was the first wave of recruitments after nationalization. Then, for the next 25 years or so, there was practically no recruitment.

The second wave of massive recruitments happened between 2010 and 2020. This second wave was mainly necessitated by the *en masse* retirements of a large majority of personnel recruited in the first wave. In the absence of sufficient number of vacancies in the various grades, the retirees belonging to the first wave did not get the benefit of regular vertical movement in their careers which they would surely have aspired for. One can imagine the kind of damage this would have caused to their morale and motivation.

The large number of retirements in banks between 2010-2020 created unexpectedly large number of vacancies at various levels. Banks had no choice but to fast-track promotions to meet this exigency. The major beneficiaries of this situation were the personnel from among those who were recruited during the 'second wave' of recruitment. This fortunate section of bank personnel or 'the early birds' (my own coinage) were soon occupying the positions of senior manager, chief manager, and assistant general manager within an unbelievably short span of 10-12 years.

While fast-track promotions *per se* are not bad, one negative aspect of it deserves mention here because of its importance. Ideally, anyone holding a position of responsibility should have had adequate experience at various levels, not just in the operational areas but also, in leadership roles before he is promoted to the next level of the hierarchy. Many of the 'early birds' lacked that kind of experience and this often adversely affected their performance. The anomalous situation brought about by long gaps in recruitments is not likely to go away till there is a system in banks to conduct recruitments matching vacancies and additional requirements at regular intervals.

HR practices to reflect the social transformation

The rapidity of social transformation driven by digitalization and intrusion of social media is mind-boggling. The onboarding of generation Z, born between 1995 and 2010, with their distinct behavioural and characteristic features, has already started in every area of life and work. This generation of people has their own opinions on everything. They do not cling to the outmoded family, social and political mores and courageously question them. The future of the banks lies in their hands.

It is estimated that by 2030 the percentage of Gen Z personnel in the global workforce will be about 33%. Rather than finding balance between work and life, they try to integrate the two. Since that is not always easy, they tend to change jobs frequently. No wonder, some of the companies in India and abroad already provide enough means of relaxation and rest within their offices, in order to cater to the needs of Gen Z employees. Improving the incentives and facilities offered to employees is another time-tested way to retain the employees. Banks need to pay special attention to the mental make-up of Gen Z employees if they wish to groom them for leadership roles in the future. In this context, the South Indian Bank's philosophy of 'Happy workers breed happy customers' and the initiative taken by them to build an inclusive management team is worth emulating. ***(Please read "Transformational Saga of South Indian Bank", Chapter 16).*** This kind of approach enhances emotional unity and the feeling of security among the staff to a considerable extent.

Relevance of the Indian ethos

We are overly fond of emulating the American style of management, which adores the smart, flamboyant and larger-than-life culture. This approach focuses mainly on maximizing power, position, income, profit and wealth with limited emphasis on human connections and humane considerations. As a result, the workforce may get more and more alienated. Our timeless scriptures like the *Mahabharata, Bhagavad Gita* and the *Ramayana* are replete with leadership insights and lessons based on compassion and trust. They are still relevant for the problem-solving needs of professionals, businessmen and ordinary individuals. Realizing this, many of our premier management training institutes like the IIMs make extensive use of the wisdom and insights found in the *Bhagavad Gita*, when they teach management lessons and ideas.

Banks need leaders, not just managers

Most of the branch managers and bank officers today are trained to be just managers, not leaders. In fact, we have the best workforce on the job. However, everywhere, people are concerned about the short-term results. This calls for a radical change at every level of the organization. The future of banking system largely lies in the synergic commitment and mutually reinforcing support of the lower, middle and top management. All of them must strive to develop the positive leadership qualities mentioned in Chapter 1.

Since leadership qualities need to be instilled and nurtured right from an early age, it is high time, our education system initiates the efforts for the development of soft skills like communication, negotiation, public speaking and principle-oriented leadership qualities among the students during the formative period of their lives.

Today, the workforce of all banks has more or less the same level of education, same level of talent, same range of age-groups and almost the same working conditions. Yet, the individual banks perform differently - some above average, some average and others below average. This clearly points to the importance of instilling leadership competence among the workforce.

Top Bureaucracy and Branch Banking

Leadership excellence needs to be institutionalized as a part of the industry's culture. To this end, high-ranking officials of the Union Finance Ministry, Reserve Bank of India and the controlling offices of the banks themselves could pay random visits to branches to see how they are working, the quality of leadership available, the areas requiring improvement etc. Getting a feel of the challenges of modern practical banking, directly from branches will be a refreshing experience to those in the corridors of power and this will also provide them valuable insights to use while formulating policies. This kind of interaction is especially necessary because the departments and regulatory bodies controlling banking today are functioning in silos, focusing only on their macro-level perspectives.

Hope for an optimistic Future

Futurologists predict that over the next decade, the scale of technological disruptions witnessed would be quite massive and unprecedented in human history. Artificial Intelligence (AI), Machine learning, Internet of things etc will cause joblessness for the workforce on an unprecedented scale, resulting in huge economic and political upheavals. It has been estimated that there will be nearly 2 million bank job losses in US and UK alone in the foreseeable future. To meet the challenges that this unpredictably disruptive scenario is likely to throw up, our banks have to reimagine the outmoded management systems, methods and strategies currently used and come up with suitable alternatives. This cannot happen without leadership excellence at every level of an organization. The sooner we start working in this direction, the better it will be. There is no time to lose.

CHAPTER 3

Reimagining Organisational Structure

"If you have a hierarchy, you're repeating the strengths and weaknesses of one person without allowing for the accumulative strength of a group."
-Gloria Steinem

The tall and flat organisation structures

Conventionally, big organizations are designed like a pyramidal hierarchical structure which follows the army type of 'command-and-control' management style. The banking system in India too has been following the aforesaid structure right from the earliest days. Under the existing pyramidal hierarchical system there are three basic layers. The first layer, top executive leadership really runs and the directs the banking organisation. The middle layer acts as facilitators who helps the juniors to do their jobs better way by discussing problems, giving advices etc, rather than telling them what to do. The third layer comprises of frontline junior managers/officers are those who really execute the banking work.

Under this structure, the branch heads and every executive above them in the hierarchy progressively assume more and more powers, depending upon their grades. This has been seen to lead to a glaring disconnect between the top executives and those at the bottom of the pyramid. Although, the boss can create a positive connection with his subordinates, the in-built tight control and supervision curbs the freedom of those manning the operational level of the hierarchical structure. Given this, there is always room for conflict situations to emerge. That apart, this kind of over centralised command structure tends to leave little room for the wealth of talent and creativity available at the frontlines to bloom and contribute to the development of a bank. However, with minimal modifications to the existing structure, the banks can still manage to tap and use all that talent and creativity. Let us find out how.

Meaning of flat organizational structure

A flat organizational structure is one where the top management is in direct contact with the operational level or front-line officers and employees who deal with the customers. This is a decentralized structure where everyone is expected to be proficient in handling whatever work comes his or her way. The branch manager or the leader supervises the employees who look upon him for support, guidance and direction. This structure has very few levels of hierarchy; it emphasises teamwork and customer focus. The superior has enough scope for delegation and decentralization of functions. A flat structure does not envisage close supervision and control but it offers the team members enough freedom to do what is good to the organisation. It instils attitudinal changes among them to scale greater heights of performance.

As the levels of hierarchy are less, downward and upward communication becomes more effective under the flat structure. It also offers the advantages of decentralized decision making, effective supervision and growth. On the HR front, it enhances the feeling of togetherness, ownership attitude, sense of freedom and personal satisfaction among the team members. As the world-renowned and highly respected management 'Guru', Peter Drucker put it, "The modern organisation cannot be an organisation of boss and subordinate. It must be organised as a team."

In the flat organisational model, groups are structured like a cricket or football team, in contrast to an army infantry which follows the command-and-control model. As the team members act as leaders as well as the front-line workers, the vertical control is remarkably reduced. The flat structure renders some designations, grades, ranks and their respective scales meaningless. This aspect needs to be suitably handled to reap benefits of the flat structure to the maximum. Apart from this, such a structure ensures that the team members are consistently energized and empowered to focus on how best they can contribute their share to the team's productivity, performance and organisational strength.

Benefits of flat structure

A flat structure facilitates relatively faster and more independent decisions as the number of layers through which a file passes is now reduced. The average bank employee today is intellectually smarter than his counterpart of the earlier generation. Therefore, he is quick on the uptake. As a result, the need for close supervision is less today than in earlier times. But, in order to draw out the best from these employees, the superior must improve his trust level with them and take active interest in their career development. He must also mentor and inspire them by example.

As the mid-level hierarchy is likely to be compressed under the flat structure, the communication flow will become easier and chances of miscommunication will be considerably reduced. Besides, employees have been found to display more sense of responsibility as also better collaboration and co-operation under the flat structure. Last but not the least, the compression is likely to result in redundancies at various levels and help the banks to save on staff expenses.

Though, such a shift could be an elaborate and time-consuming exercise, it is worth a serious consideration by the banks keeping in mind the benefits to be reaped. Even if a 100% shift to the flat structure is not practicable, the pyramidal hierarchy can at least be converted to a near-flat structure.

Need for compression of scales

Currently, banks have in place the following scales and corresponding categories of posts: scale VII and VI top executive grades, Scale V and IV senior management grades, Scale III and II middle management grades and Scale I junior management grade. The seven grades dispensation based on the recommendations of the Pillai Committee came into effect in 1979. This system was suitable when the banks were fully operated in manual mode. However, In the fast-changing digital scenario of today, multi-dimensional scales like the above are no longer relevant. Since, all the banks have been fully computerized and networked, there is room for suitably compressing the existing structure *after conducting necessary studies.* For instance, some public sector banks have recently brought the field general managers to their banks' headquarters, by undertaking rationalization of some Bank branches. Similarly, banks can rethink continuation of some layers in the senior and middle management. The shrinking of hierarchy into relatively flat structure, will bring the bosses closer to employees down. The resulting vertical movement of relatively younger staff working on the frontlines is bound to be motivated to give their best for the development of the banks. It is not a necessary that the same system has to be continued indefinitely for ages. The die-hard habits and traditional systems are to be replaced by newly gained knowledge and experience. In other words, future changes shall be holistic and not patchy or piecemeal.

Cluster heads

With the increasing number of branches and exponential growth of business, the regional offices of many banks find themselves saddled with too many administrative problems. In order to tide over the hurdles faced by the regional offices, some of the private banks have started resorting to the 'cluster' approach. Under this approach, banks post 'cluster heads' to oversee the functioning and business growth of the branches on a day-to-day basis. Some private sector banks like HDFC and South Indian Bank are among those who have adopted this approach currently.

Cluster head is the immediate first-layer supervisory contact-point of the branches. They are normally a select group of officers with proven competence and branch-managing experience. A cluster head, who are directly under Regional Office, supervises an average of 10-12 branches. The branches have to report to the cluster heads who in turn will report directly to their regional heads. They are expected to hasten the all-round growth and development of the branches. The outstanding ones among the cluster-heads can expect to be rewarded by promotion to the position of regional heads.

Cluster heads are stationed in any one of the city branches for administrative reasons. They occasionally visit the branches under their jurisdiction. They maintain continuous contact with the branch level functionaries and ensure rapid growth and development of the branches under their watch. Their high leadership attributes and competencies enable them to inspire the branch managers and the staff to perform to the new level of excellence. Creating the post of cluster heads for strengthening the administrative system at the regional level, is a step in the right direction. The organisation should consistently motivate the cluster heads to function as effective team leaders.

Cluster heads are expected to possess extraordinary leadership qualities and help the employees to connect to the organisation emotionally. They must remember that the entire organisational exercise can be viewed as a game where the employees are the team players. Like a cricket or football team, the team leader should ensure that his team wins ultimately. Success of one or two players will not mean the team's success. Eventually, the successful and synergistic performance of all the players in the team and the performance excellence of all the cluster heads in the bank will lead to the success of the organization as a whole. Winning should be the central goal of all in the teams. He creates a win-win situation for everyone - something like the legendary cricketer Sachin Tendulkar on the of his 50th birthday said, " Till the end of my career, it did not matter who was the captain...... I will do the same role irrespective of whether I am a captain or not. I'll still be like a leader, because I believe you need to have 11 leaders on the field."

How a cluster head could inspire team members?

Ideally, a cluster head should not be just another officer. He must be an officer with substance and a leader with purpose. He should be a friend, philosopher and guide of the team, having warmth and friendliness. He must be resilient and be able to convince and influence his team that life and work are complementary and not competitive. An effective cluster head will not only like to be a winner himself but will also like to see his team and his organization win when he wins. As an ideal team-leader the cluster head must win the hearts of the team members. The best example of team-based leadership qualities is the exciting performance of the famous cricketer M.S.Dhoni, 'Mr Cool', the cynosure of cricket lovers around the world, displayed in the cricketing world for many years before stepping down from the captaincy of the Indian cricket team. ***(Please also read Annexure II ("Leadership Excellence -The Taj way").***

CHAPTER 4

The Challenges Of Managing Credit Portfolio: Some Basic Steps To Become A Good Credit Officer

The challenges of managing the credit portfolio are manifold. It is therefore essential that a credit officer has the necessary mental equipment to deal with them in a professional manner. For better understanding, I would like to discuss the competencies expected of a credit officer in two parts. The first part is about the competencies needed to address some of the internal aspects of credit management while the second part deals with the competencies needed to address some external factors.

INTERNAL ASPECTS OF CREDIT MANAGEMENT

Mastering the fundamentals

The credit officers, whether working in the branch or in the separate credit verticals, can handle their work with confidence only if they possess sufficient knowledge and skills to do their job. In other words, domain expertise is most important for a credit officer. It may require months and years of sustained work and effort to acquire it. To begin with, credit officers must be familiar with all the systems and procedures obtaining in their bank. They must also possess high-level analytical ability and outstanding capacity to communicate, negotiate and unearth the details of the borrower's ***character, capacity and capital***, from direct and indirect sources. They must regularly read the circulars issued by their controlling offices, RBI and other regulatory bodies. They should be regularly going through economic dailies and magazines etc to update and sharpen their existing knowledge. The types of credit facilities generally offered by the banks are: fund-based credit facilities like cash credits, overdrafts, demand loans, discounting of bills, retail credit etc and non-fund-based credit facilities like letters of credit, bank guarantees, deferred payment guarantees etc. The credit requirements of a business enterprise generally are working capital, for meeting day-to-day operations and fixed capital for acquiring land and building, plant and machinery etc.

Normally, the branch has to collect application for the loan in their prescribed forms from the individuals or business units seeking credit facilities. In the case of business units, along with various other prescribed documents, copies of income tax returns, balance sheets and cash flow details for the past three years are to be collected. They should be analysed in detail, as a prelude to sanctioning the loan. Once the loan is sanctioned, the officers concerned (whether in the branch or in the retail asset hubs) must strictly comply with the prescribed documentation and carry out necessary monitoring and follow-up for recovery depending on the status of an account, without any deviation from the prescribed guidelines. In a nutshell, credit management deals with the processing of credit proposals covering analysis of financial ratios and project appraisal, sanctioning and releasing of credit, credit monitoring, following prescribed recovery measures including filing of suit etc. Every Bank normally will have its Manual of Instructions and a series of circulars issued from time to time, which may contain the guidelines to be followed by employees while discharging their duties. As mentioned earlier, to become a good credit officer, one must possess a thorough understanding of these guidelines and also possess personal qualities like honesty, integrity and sincerity, insight and a basic understanding of human psychology to deal with different types of borrowers.

Adherence to the principles of lending

The timeless principles of sound lending are ***safety, liquidity and profitability***. Safety first should always be the guiding norm. In other words, the lender should ensure that the amount advanced must come back with interest within the repayment period stipulated. There are well-established systems, rules and policies/procedures followed by a banker to assess the security and cash flows, to determine source of repayments and to evaluate the creditworthiness of the borrower. The last-mentioned exercise has been considerably facilitated by the setting up of the Credit Information Bureau of India (CIBIL). CIBIL was formed on May 5, 2004 for the purpose of sharing factual credit information reports on the credit history and repayment records of commercial and consumer borrowers with the member-banks. It helps the banks to take informed, objective and speedy credit decisions and thereby curb the rise of Non-Performing Assets (NPAs).

The appraisal process

In the case of term loans, bankers have to appraise technical, commercial, managerial and financial aspects of a project in detail. Technical appraisal is the study of availability of basic infrastructure, licensing/registration requirements, selection of technology, availability of raw materials and skilled labour etc. Under commercial appraisal, the focus is on analysing and assessing the information on demand and supply-current and projected, distribution, pricing, market etc. Under managerial appraisal, the banker tries to figure out the details of ***three Cs-Character, Capacity and Capital*** of the borrower before lending. Under financial appraisal, the viability of the project (its capacity to develop and survive independently) is carefully gauged.

Financial statement analysis

The credit officers must be able to critically analyse the financial statements- Profit and Loss Account, Balance Sheet and Cash Flow Statement from different angles. The following is a thumbnail sketch of the whole exercise.

Before analysing, the balance sheet, the items therein should be grouped as necessary. Thereafter, one should establish the relationship between one item or group of items in the balance sheet or P&L a/c, and another item or group of items by arriving at ratios that express their relationship in mathematical terms. In simple terms, a ratio is the quotient obtained by dividing the value of one variable in the financial statements by the value of another variable. In some cases, a comparison of values under the same variable for different years may be necessitated in order to understand the trend over a period of time. Here, the changes would be expressed in terms of year-to-year percentage changes during the relevant period. The quantitative data need to be interpreted in a qualitative way to help ascertain the direction in which the firm is moving. A painstaking and thorough analysis normally throws sufficient light on the strengths and weaknesses of a business enterprise, to help decision-making on the part of the credit sanctioning authority.

Broadly there are four categories of ratios: liquidity, leverage or capital structure, activity and profitability ratios. They help one to get an idea of the viability, stability, turnover and profitability respectively of a firm. For example, to assess a credit proposal for sanction of cash credit or overdraft facility, it is important to find out the liquidity ratios like current ratio, acid-test ratio and cash ratios of the applicant as they signify his ability to meet short-term commitments. For a term loan, knowing the leverage ratios is important. Debt equity ratio is of one of the leverage ratios which helps to measure the relative proportions of a firm's debt and equity used to finance the assets. The ratio helps to assess the promoter's stake and gauge the risks in advancing funds to a firm. While the stock turnover ratio is used for ascertaining the sales turnover, profitability ratios are used to assess the profitability of a firm. Debt Service Coverage ratio helps to find out its capacity to service debt obligations. Similarly, cash flow analysis helps discern the adequacy or otherwise of the flow of money in the organisation over a period of time.

Now-a-days, computerized financial statement analysis software is readily available. If the balance sheet data are fed into the computer, one can get the results of the analyses instantly. Nevertheless, it is always good to have an in-depth understanding of the dynamics of ratio analysis.

Regulatory changes

Income Recognition and Asset Classification (IRAC) norms and deregulation of interest rates were two important changes brought into Indian banking in the beginning of the 1990's. In later years, the old accounting standards were scrapped and new accounting standards were introduced in their place. All these changes were effected so as to make credit assessment and decision-making processes finer and more objective. The credit officer and the branch-head must equip themselves with the necessary knowledge to cope with such changes.

Lending then and now

We live in an era where change is the only constant in any walk of life. Back in the mid-1970s when this writer started his banking career, life was relatively simpler. People were generally averse to taking loans from banks. Availing a bank loan was reflective of the poor financial capacity of a person. Dishonesty and delinquency among borrowers were not rampant yet. The average borrower normally played it straight. KYC norms and money laundering were unheard of in those days. Come the late 1990's, businesses and the economy started thriving. But, so did manipulative tendencies among a section of borrowers who were ever on the look-out for more and more clever ways to cheat banks. No wonder that this period saw a number of cases of banks being swindled by unscrupulous characters to the tune of crores of rupees in fraudulent ways like manipulation of property documents offered as security for real estate/housing loans, securing discounting of bills with fake Lorry receipts/Railway receipts etc.

Vulnerability of Bank Officers

Loans are granted to borrowers for a variety of purposes ranging from tiding over a temporary financial difficulty to buying a fixed asset to enhance the productive capacity of a firm. Without such loans, the wheels of commerce and industry could grind to a halt. For the lending banks too, such loans are extremely important as they yield sizeable interest income. Once a borrower's financial position improves, he normally reduces his dependence on bank loans. Unfortunately, today, this ideal situation can be found only in rare cases and a borrower's dependence on his banker is increasingly becoming a lifelong process, in most cases. Given this and the all-too-frequent changes in the economic scenario, the number of cases of Non-Performing Assets (NPAs) too has gone up. Needless to say, in such a situation, a banker must exercise due diligence and care while lending.

Transparency of data

In order to formulate strategic planning exercises, correct data for a particular period are needed at CO/HO level. Banks must eschew the practices of relying on old or wrong data. Ensuring transparency, as clear as sunlight, is always the best policy. To this end, practices like window-dressing and ever-greening of loan accounts should be strictly avoided. Any breach of terms and conditions with regard to loans advanced must be brought to the notice of the higher authorities without delay and corrective action initiated at the earliest.

Organised customer education

Indian banking system has contributed immensely to the development of Indian economy and blossoming of the lives of people hitherto neglected. In the mutual interests of banks and their customers, encouraging financial literacy among customers through customer education initiatives is a worthy goal for banks to pursue. Such education can be imparted to school and college students as well, as they are the future citizens of this country. Let us look at one example of how such initiatives can help banks as well as their customers. Some borrowers are ignorant, careless and complacent of how to handle their debts. In such cases, the chances of their account turning irregular are high. When these accounts become doubtful or loss assets, the banks send possession notice under SARFAESI Act 2002 to the borrowers/ guarantors. In the event of continued default, the assets are taken over and sold within 60 days from the date of the receipt of the notice. In the light of the foregoing, timely repayment of loan instalments could be one of the points that could be highlighted during customer education programmes. This will not only spare the borrower from overdue interest and other penal charges but also the other problems that continued default brings. Needless to say, this would also mean reduction in the number of delinquent accounts for the banks to handle; a win-win situation for both sides.

EXTERNAL FACTORS

Banking is a major component of the financial ecosystem of the country. While it influences the other components of the financial ecosystem, the converse is also true. In other words, while a number of components of the financial ecosystem are influenced by developments under banking, banking itself is influenced by developments under some of the other components. Additionally, in this era of Liberalisation, Privatisation and

Globalisation (LPG), banking is also influenced by political and economic developments abroad. In order to do justice to his job, a credit officer needs to keep abreast of such developments too. A few of these external factors, illustrative not exhaustive, are discussed below.

1. Rate of inflation

The rate of inflation in an economy has direct bearing on the interest rates which in turn directly affect the income earned by a bank. A banker therefore needs to carefully monitor the inflationary trends in the economy.

2. GDP trends

Normally, when the Gross Domestic Product of a country is rising, most sectors of an economy are seen to be doing well. For any banker, that gives a kind of reassurance while taking a lending decision.

3. CRR and SLR

These statutory controls wielded by Reserve Bank of India decide to a large extent the availability of lendable funds with banks. Normally, these rates are increased when the Reserve Bank of India wants to restrict the supply of money. Conversely, when RBI is following a policy of monetary expansion, these rates are lowered.

4. Trade matters

India is a member of the WTO (World Trade Organization). The fact that India has only limited options as far as restricting imports from other countries is concerned has serious implications for indigenous producers of various products. Unlike in earlier times, these producers have to contend with not only local competition but also the competition from overseas sellers. In view of this, before financing a unit operating in a highly competitive market, a bank needs to thoroughly assess the unit's ability to withstand such competition without compromising on its profitability.

5. Exchange rates

Exchange rates play a significant role in the export competitiveness of a country. For example, the exchange value of Indian Rupee against U.S. Dollar has been consistently going down during the last few months.

This would make an Indian exporter's products cheaper for his overseas buyers. To that extent, his products become more competitive abroad. At the same time, for an importer in India, the situation will be the opposite. This is because now he will have to pay more in rupee terms for his imports. A bank should be to understand the impact of these changes on the business of his borrower-customer for only then can he avoid taking unnecessary risks while lending.

6. The state of Indian agriculture

Agriculture is risky business and the farmers are heavily dependent on loans to cultivate. If they are not assured of reasonable income, farming becomes still more risky. Agricultural advances form a major component of the credit portfolio of any Indian bank. Due to this reason, it is essential that a credit officer has a basic understanding of the various problems faced by the farmer. Major problems faced by Indian agriculture can be summed up as: Too many people depending on agriculture, inadequate irrigation and storage facilities, small and fragmented holdings, scarcity of quality seeds, lack of marketing support, absence of mechanism to ensure remunerative prices, scarcity of fertilisers and manures, limited use of machines, dwindling of water table due to over-exploitation of underground water etc.

A detailed discussion of these problems may take an entire book. However, for the purpose of this chapter, a look at the following list should be enough to give one an idea of the range and magnitude of these problems.

1. The use of technology

The use of digital technology has changed the face of Indian banking in recent years. This has helped banks to improve their efficiency and customer service. It has reduced their cost of operations and enabled them to have in place better information and communication systems. A banker should be ever on the look-out for ways to harness the limitless possibilities offered by digital technology to stay ahead of the competition.

2. The bane of consumerism

The relentless pursuit of self-gratification of the people, the emergence of a powerful middle class with insatiable desire for various products and services and the changing attitude of the average Indian towards borrowing heralded the arrival of the age of consumerism in India in the 1990s. They forget that when pursuit of wealth becomes an end in itself, life becomes stagnant and meaningless. In this context let me recall Elise Boulding who said, "The consumption society has made us feel that happiness lies in having things, and has failed to teach us the happiness of not having things."

This is not to say that one should not have any needs. Let me elaborate. The need for a house of one's own is legitimate. But, it becomes problematic when one wants to buy a palatial house to keep up with the Joneses or just to impress one's friends and relatives. When such tendencies take hold of a person, he may waste money often, trying to be what he is not. The availability of bank loans could further encourage such abnormal tendencies in him. And, if he manages to get a loan, the result could be overstretching of the family budget leading to default in repayment and the account becoming an NPA.

3. Need for developing sense of discrimination for a healthy and sustainable credit culture

The credit officers and the branch managers should develop the sense to distinguish a loan proposal born out of a genuine need from other proposals which are prompted merely by an urge to compete with someone or the habit of one-upmanship. A banker should use his persuasive skills to discourage the second kind of loan proposals. It may be noted that reckless borrowing is not done by individuals alone. Even businessmen and corporates sometimes get into debt-traps in pursuit of their over-ambitious plans to expand their businesses or to capture new markets. The outcome in such cases is rarely happy. There are even cases where such people committed suicide out of desperation. This point has been further elaborated in the form of a real-life case study for the benefit of the readers ***(Refer Annexure III Bitten by the bug of consumerism).***

4. Digital loan apps (DLAs)

Digital loan apps of social media firms are fast growing platform to offer small size retail credit. According to a Parliamentary committee report of 2023, the digital lending in India grew 39.5% annually between 2012 and 2023 to touch $350 billion. However, the RBI study over 2 months January and February 2021, found that out of 1100 loan apps, 600 were illegal. The DLAs are attractive because of its convenience financing. In urgency, people can get the loan easily; however, interest rates are far higher than banks'.

Police investigations reveal that shady loan apps are downloaded to phones, illegally copy borrowers' phone data and the same is used to harass the debtors when the repayments are delayed. The morphed photos of the borrowers are sent to all numbers on their phone list which has even led to suicides. There should be on-going public awareness campaigns and the fast prosecution for criminality. The regulated financial intermediaries are required to make it easier for retail borrowers to approach them. Banking system is highly sensitive to the entire economy. The bankers must understand that a problem in one bank can immediately undermine confidence in the entire system.

5. Need for credit counselling

When a bank opens up credit to start jobs and invest in business, it unlocks huge economic power for the borrowers, other people and for the whole economy. Bank credit is a lifeline which can do wonders if properly handled. But when debt becomes unsustainable, it could mean the difference between life and death for a borrower. Unless used in a disciplined way, the debt may ruin individual and families, organisations or even nations. In these days of orchestrated consumerism, debt has become a hype, fashion and inalienable part of people's lives. The analogy what the doctors used to say, "Medicine *per se* is not bad, but lifelong medication is dangerous" is highly relevant in this context. The debtor's position is not anyway different from this.

Though there are huge number of good and honest borrowers who make most out of the debt, it is important that bankers re-imagine and redefine their roles in the context of the complexities of the times and act accordingly, if they want to stay relevant. For instance, they can regularly sensitize the potential and existing borrowers about the positive and negative consequences of living in debt. They may be counselled to distinguish that the loan for doing business is productive and self-liquidating in nature, whereas a bank loan for conspicuous consumption is non-productive and not self-liquidating. Banks can conduct extensive research analysis on the data of delinquent borrowers; the valuable information of their behavioural pattern thus gained can be profitably used in future.

Banks need not worry about the potential loss of borrowers due to such sensitization efforts as debt requirements will remain in the market forever. Moreover, the borrowers may view the well-meaning counselling efforts of the banks as an empathetic gesture, which may eventually lead to a win-win situation for both. Let the modern bankers may create and recreate paradigm shifts in professionalism with a human touch.

....

CHAPTER 5

Communication : The Leadership Way

"The most important thing in communication is to hear what isn't being said.
-Peter Drucker

Multiple skills determine and shape our development and the success in life. Communication which is the most fundamental, ranks top among them. Communication skills are to be developed and continually refined by all leaders. It helps to improve relationships, resolve conflicts, maintain harmony and ensure peaceful co-existence within the family as well as work and social environments. In the domain of management, Peter Drucker father of modern management, says that 60% of all the management problems are the result of faulty communication.

Banking is a service oriented. While a department store or a retail trader deals in physical products, a banker deals in services products. Two important features of services products are intangibility and inseparability. While physical products, for instance, car, refrigerator, items of furniture, washing machine, sugar and rice are tangible, services products such as fixed deposit, cash credit limit, recurring deposit, involving different kinds of services are not tangible. The second feature of 'inseparability' follows from the first one, namely, 'intangibility'. A tangible and visible product can stand on its own and therefore, a prospective buyer can try to assess whether it is good enough to buy or not, by looking at it or touching it or tasting it or test-driving it (in the case of cars), subject to the consent of the seller and decide accordingly. However, the services products are inseparable from the persona of the seller. In other words, the personality of the seller, his behaviour, his ability to communicate and convince, his empathy and concern for others etc. are going to be as important as the features of the relevant product. The importance of communication skills in banking should be evident from the foregoing. The basic forms of communication are: Reading, Writing, Speaking and Listening. Speaking and listening become more effective when they are combined with appropriate body language and gestures. Let us now discuss the various aspects of communication in detail.

READING

Reading makes you well-informed, creative, refined and cultured. It also helps to improve your language and enhance your confidence by adding value to your professional competence. Sadly, with the arrival of social media, reading habit has been on the wane everywhere. One may chat, play games or watch movies and read news/current affairs in capsule form on his mobile phone but he hardly finds any time for serious reading. What a pity considering that information technology is a great boon if used to broaden and deepen our knowledge! As a banker, you should not only be regularly reading newspapers, economic dailies, circulars issued by RBI and your bank, but also widening, deepening and updating your knowledge with the help of internet. It is not an option, but a compelling necessity.

How to read effectively?

In order to make reading effective, it is always better to read slowly first, followed by a second reading to make your understanding clearer. However, the aforesaid method may not suit those who are perennially short of time. Such people could try the Skimming and Scanning techniques of reading.

Skimming

Skimming is the process of reading only the main ideas contained in each paragraph to get an overall idea of the content. It involves the following steps:

a) Read the title.
b) Read the introduction or the first paragraph.
c) Read the first sentence of the other paragraphs and the headings and sub-headings.
d) Take note of the emphasis given to certain words and sentences

through bold font or italics.
e) Read the summary or the last paragraph.

Scanning

Scanning is a reading technique used to find specific information about a matter from a passage which not only contains the required information but also those unrelated to the matter. For this, the information-seeker must be clear about what specific information he is looking for. If he has any clues to guide him, so much the better.

Reading requires concentration, without which one cannot remember the details. What one reads should be understood and internalized so that it could be retrieved later, when needed. Otherwise, the purpose of reading will be defeated. After one has read a book mindfully for half an hour or so, one should stop for about 10 minutes to review what was read and then proceed. This method will reinforce one's memory of what was read and ensure effective reading.

WRITING

While the ability to read well and speak well can be acquired with reasonable amount of effort and dedication, writing well requires effort and dedication of a higher order spread over a longer period of time. In other words, compared with reading and speaking, writing is a comparatively a more difficult skill to acquire. To write clearly, one needs to be able to think clearly. Without clarity of thought, your message may confuse the readers instead of informing or educating them. Regularly reading newspapers, periodicals and books and noting down original and interesting ways of expression used by authors and looking up the dictionary for meanings of unfamiliar words and idioms etc. are necessary steps for developing one's writing ability. After acquiring the basic writing skills, one may try writing articles, essays etc. and send them to newspapers or magazines for publication. If they are good enough, they will get published. If they are not, one should not become despondent. Instead, the rejection should be used to motivate oneself to work harder.

Writing letters

In an organisational set-up, one is expected to write different types of letters, the bulk of which may relate to commercial and business matters. The main features of a good letter are a) Accuracy, (b) Brevity and (c) Clarity (ABC). As mentioned earlier, clarity of thought and purpose is an important pre-requisite for good writing. The letters should be short and simple and so worded as to arouse curiosity of the reader. As far as possible, one should avoid including more than one idea in a paragraph and use simple yet power-packed and meaningful words to communicate. Like a sculptor who chisels his sculpture again and again to make it beautiful and expressive, one should follow the 'less is more' approach while writing. Care should be taken to use the correct salutation e.g. Dear Sir, Dear Mr. Ram and the correct subscription e.g. Yours faithfully, Yours truly, while writing a letter. Never write a reply when you are angry or feeling uncomfortable for some reason. Likewise, don't make any commitment when you are feeling extremely happy. These can turn out to be entrapping moments if not handled carefully and may cost you dearly. One should think twice before committing oneself to any course of action at such times. It is always good to remember that "Haste makes waste"

Writing reports, analysis etc

Many a time, branch heads may have to prepare notes/reports on several issues relating to the performance of their branch, for submission to higher offices. As a branch manager when you prepare a report to explain to your Regional Manager on your failure to adhere to the norms while sanctioning a particular credit facility to a certain customer, the language to be used should be clear and precise. It is common to see branch managers taking up to 10-12 pages to say something which could easily be compressed into 1-2 pages. Long winding and convoluted letters are best avoided as this may result in the subject matter not getting timely attention from the receiver.

Issue of Head Office Circulars

From time to time, various departments of a bank at the head office and other administrative offices have to circularise guidelines, instructions etc. relating to various matters for the information of branches. As far as possible, circulars should be drafted in direct, clear and concise language. For the sake of clarity and cross check, it is advisable to quote the reference numbers and dates of the earlier circulars issued on the same topic. A circular issued by the head office or any other controlling office of a bank is treated as the authorised and final version of whatever is contained therein. Banks normally preserve the circulars as permanent records since they may have to be produced before the courts or the regulatory authorities any time for a variety of reasons. Considering the importance of the circulars, they should be got printed only after ensuring that they are free from errors or mistakes. However, despite all the precautionary measures, it may so happen that factual or other kinds of errors may sometimes get detected in such circulars after they are dispatched to the branches. In such cases, a corrigendum should be issued and circulated without delay.

Electronic communication

In this era of electronic communication, communicating through e-mails or SMS messages and chatting on WhatsApp, Telegram, Facebook Messenger etc is common. E-mails are used for detailed communication. It is a simple and flexible mode of communication. It can be used for asking questions and getting answers, making people aware of issues, passing on information, sending copies of documents etc. Chatting is a way of engaging in informal or friendly conversation over phone with friends. SMS is used for sending short messages from one mobile phone to another. As of now, WhatsApp is the most popular messaging app worldwide. It offers real-time text transmission via Internet. Since the arrival of smart phones, the low-cost and free-chat messaging apps like WhatsApp, Weixin/Wechat, Facebook Messenger, Snapchat etc have proven themselves to be cheaper and more efficient alternatives to the operator-based text messaging via SMS. Electronic communication has replaced the conventional method of sending letters by post to a considerable extent. Accuracy, brevity, clarity and simplicity should be the hallmarks of electronic communication. It should be noted that electronic communication must be used very responsibly as any mishandling of the medium can have grave repercussions.

Videoconferencing is another highly cost-effective medium used by companies for communication between the top management of the organization and functionaries at lower levels. When communication is activated in the faster electronic mode, decision-making and other processes also tend to become faster and more efficient. Properly managed, use of electronic communication can neutralise corruption, lethargy and bureaucratic delays to a great extent.

LISTENING

Listening is one of the major elements of communication. This is an area of weakness for many people. When you listen intently to another person, he begins to develop confidence in you. Sometimes, even if you are not able to listen to something completely, it would be enough to try and grasp the main points. Many times, prejudice against the speaker is the reason behind poor listening. Adhering to the following guidelines helps one become a good listener.

1. When the other person is speaking, one should give full attention to what he is saying.
2. Make it a point to make the other person feel welcome and free to talk.
3. Act and look interested in what the other person is going to say. Keep eye contact and give appropriate non-verbal responses when the other person is talking.
4. Don't shuffle papers or tap on the table or look down.
5. Empathize or place yourself in the shoes of the talker and try to understand his point of view.
6. Be patient and give sufficient time to the other person to talk. Do not interrupt.
7. Avoid becoming angry at anything said. An angry man is likely to misunderstand even harmless words or sentences.
8. Avoid arguments and criticism: Such responses can make the talker angry or make him shut up.
9. Asking relevant questions is a positive signal to the talker that you are listening. It helps to keep the conversation going and sometimes, brings out in the open unexplored aspects of a topic.

Empathetic listening

Empathetic listening is the highest form of listening. It is through empathy that we internalize another person's heart and mind and silently experience the feelings and experience of another person. It is not listening with ears alone, but with eyes and hearts. It is through empathetic listening that we can try to accurately understand the internal frame of reference of another person. Internal frame of reference includes the range of inner feelings and perceptions sensed by an individual.

When a person starts talking, the foremost thing required is to listen in silence. As Lady Dorothy Nevill says, "The real art of conversation is not only to say the right thing in the right place, but to leave unsaid the wrong thing at the tempting moment."

SPEAKING

Speaking skills are very important for any human being as without them it is difficult to communicate with other human beings in any situation, be it within the family or with friends or with unknown people. Depending on who we are speaking to, our speech may be formal or informal. Formal speaking is necessary at the workplace or while speaking to unknown people. For speaking to family members and friends, we use the informal way of speaking. There are four elements in speaking skills : Vocabulary, Grammar, Pronunciation and Fluency. In order to be a good speaker, one must be good in all the four elements. Otherwise, there is always the possibility of miscommunication which could result in the listener either not understanding or misunderstanding what was said by the speaker.

Conversation

Conversation is a form of interactive and spontaneous communication between two or more people who are following the rules of etiquette. Conversation can be face-to-face or online. Conversation is the basic tool for social interaction and personal success. A meaningful conversation is a great learning experience which helps to improve one's knowledge and confidence. Free and frank conversation with others makes a person feel at ease and develop intimacy and warmth towards others leading to good interpersonal relations. Given below are some tips to make conversations effective.

(i) Holding conversations face-to-face is always more effective than having it online as the former enables the parties involved to not just hear what the other person is saying but also, see and feel it.
(ii). It is always good to know the background of the person/s you are going to talk with as this enables you to choose the level and manner to adopt for the conversation. If you are talking to ordinary people, you should come down to their level and avoid sounding pompous or unduly sophisticated.
(iii) Ensure that the atmosphere during the conversation is not tense as this may come in the way of a proper understanding of messages.
(iv) Ensure that your verbal and non-verbal communications are in sync. For example, if there is a frown on the face of a manager who intently listens to the suggestion made by a person lower down in the hierarchy, the latter may conclude that the manager is either against the suggestion or simply not interested in listening to it though the reality may be something else. Instead of frowning, one should keep an open body posture and try to nod in between listening to show the speaker that one is seriously listening to what he is saying.
(v) Scheduling of conversations is as important as the subject of the conversations. Therefore, care should be taken to schedule them in such a way that they do not upset the schedules of the others. If this cannot be totally avoided, try to ensure that the inconvenience is kept at the minimum.
(vi) Choose your words carefully and avoid foul language. Words convey feelings, emotions, pains and pleasures; their vibrations are potentially long-lasting. Therefore, ensure that choice of words is appropriate to the occasion and to the kind of people who are listening to you as otherwise, there is always the possibility of your being misunderstood or misinterpreted. And always remember that politeness, clarity, brevity and beauty of language are the soul of effective communication.

Public speaking

To be a good leader, one of the most important skills required is the ability to speak eloquently and effectively before the public. Through extensive and intensive reading consciously targeted at improving one's vocabulary and knowledge of the language and regularly engaging in writing and listening on the lines suggested earlier, one can strengthen one's overall inner confidence which is essential for public speaking.

In public speaking, unlike in a normal conversation, we are subjected to intense scrutiny by an audience which may sometimes run into hundreds or even thousands. This coupled with our fear of failure causes heightened flow of adrenalin, manifesting symptoms of nervousness like sweating palms, breathlessness, trembling hands etc. Therefore, the first step in becoming a confident speaker is to realize that this kind of nervousness happens to all who have to confront situations where they are under intense scrutiny. In order to successfully avoid nervousness and build supreme confidence, one has to make painstaking preparation before the speech, by adopting certain techniques to control the nerves. The following tips may be helpful to those who are just starting out in public speaking.

(i) Try to confine public speaking to topics well-known to you.
(ii) Collect the demographic profile like average age, average educational level etc. of the target audience to decide where to pitch your speech. Remember, a speech meant for post-graduate students should not be delivered to the students of primary classes.
(iii) Find out the time allotted to you for speaking and tailor the length of your speech accordingly.
(iv) Plan and prepare your speech well before the scheduled day. If necessary, write down your speech. Avoid memorising it word by word as if, by chance, you forget even one or two words in the midst of your speech, your mind may go blank and you will be reduced to a nervous wreck. It is ideal to remember the broad idea of the speech. The key words and phrases and the arguments/evidence must be put forward sequentially.
(v) A speech must start with an introduction, followed by the main body of the speech and the conclusion. The introduction part should begin with the salutation. A lackadaisical speech during the early phase may drift the attention of the audience elsewhere and you will lose them totally.
(vi) Dress yourself appropriately. Never wear a dress which makes you feel self-conscious.

(vii) Avoid nervousness; calm yourself by drawing in deep breaths and by clenching and unclenching your fists. Try to have a sweeping eye contact with the audience; don't stare at anyone in the audience.
(viii) Avoid stiffness and let your hands hang loosely on the sides. You may even temporarily slip your hands into the pockets of your trousers if that makes you comfortable.

Phone conversation

Communicating through landline telephones and mobile phones is an integral part of life today. The following are some tips on how to improve the quality and effectiveness of telephonic conversations.

Develop the habit of visualising or writing down the list of points that you want to speak on before making a telephone call. This way, you can speak in an orderly and systematic manner covering all points in one call without lapsing into awkward silences and wasting time on trying to figure out what to say next. If you are going to speak to someone for the first time, as soon as he/she picks up the phone, introduce yourself with due cordiality and warmth. Try to speak clearly and audibly to avoid having to repeat yourself. Avoid using speakerphone unless it is necessary. Avoid discussing personal and domestic issues on telephone. Ensure that whatever is conveyed by you is consistent and without any self-contradiction.

Use formal language as far as possible unless you are talking to someone who is intimate with you. Humour can have a place during these conversations. Avoid inappropriate jokes which could upset people. Try to remain cheerful and positive even in the face of extreme provocation from the other person. Try to answer incoming calls within three rings. If you do not have the answer to something, do not dilly-dally. Avoid shouting at anyone over the phone. If talking aloud is a must, make sure that there is no one near enough to hear you.

Body language

Body language or non-verbal communication involves neither written nor spoken words. It is generally used in conjunction with verbal communication to make the communication process more powerful and effective. As a proverb tells us, “Face is the index of the mind and eyes are the mirror of the soul”. Apart from engaging in verbal communication we also use different parts of our body to express varying emotions like anger, fear, anxiety, melancholy, shock, happiness etc. The body movements, or kinesics as they are called, include gestures, postures, facial expressions, eye contact etc.

Research shows that these non-verbal components of the body language have predictable association with certain kinds of attitudes and behaviour. For example, shifting movements of eyes while speaking is believed to signify embarrassment or lying; leaning away while speaking is believed to indicate boredom; leaning forward is believed to indicate curiosity; tapping of fingers is believed to indicate impatience; lip-biting is believed to indicate nervousness. Research by Professor Albert Mehrabian of the University of California reveals that while communicating, only 7% of the meaning is conveyed through words, 38% through tone of voice and 55% through body language. As can be seen above, body language clearly has a greater role to play in communication than the other components.

Like most things in life, the ability to communicate well cannot be acquired overnight; it may take months or even years of experience and practice before one starts getting everything right. When you encounter communication failures, try to understand what went wrong and identify the underlying reason or problem which caused it. Try to overcome it, if necessary, in consultation with an expert. As Brian Tracy, the famous author puts it “Communication is a skill that you can learn. It’s like riding a bicycle or typing. If you are willing to work at it, you can rapidly improve the quality of every part of your life.”

....

CHAPTER 6

Knowledge Management : Investing In Your Path To Success

"An investment in knowledge pays the best interest."
-Benjamin Franklin

KNOWLEDGE IS POWER

These days, to achieve power and success, we require not just knowledge, but also more knowledge about the process of learning itself. Alvin Toffler said, "Today's illiterate is not the person who doesn't know how to read and write; he is the man who has not learned how to learn." Given the aforesaid scenario, the importance of teaching oneself should be clear. Sadly, for the average youth today, "teaching oneself" is rarely a priority, given the variety of ways available to him/her to spend time on.

In the olden days, mainly wealth and muscular power symbolized the affluence of the rich. Today, knowledge is considered as important as wealth and muscular power. The reason for this is the fact that knowledge has today become the key to not just wealth and power but also to good health and the various finer aspects which lend quality to one's life. Knowledge is important not just for individuals but also for governments, institutions, organizations, businesses etc. as discussed below.

KNOWLEDGE MANAGEMENT

Why Knowledge management is important

1) To meet intense competition

Knowledge is an intangible organisational asset. Knowledge management is a concept in which an organisation gathers, stores and disseminates knowledge to the workforce systematically in order to improve their work efficiency and effectiveness. It is necessitated by the intense competition in the current globalised environment and for improving the operational efficiency of businesses and services. Therefore, the bankers too have to improve knowledge by reading, listening, collating and contemplating the information received from various sources, which should help improve their credit decisions, innovative skills and overall competencies. This can also improve their ability to guide others suitably. Almost all banks today have put in place well-equipped systems for disseminating knowledge to their workforce. Many of them have designated Chief Learning Officers to oversee knowledge management in their respective organisations. This is indicative of the increasing importance being given to the task of knowledge management by banks.

Considering the importance of knowledge management in the organizational context, it is imperative to implement the same effectively. Here, one must remember that knowledge sharing in an organization is targeted at adult learners who are normally reluctant learners. As the idiom goes, you can lead a horse to water, but you cannot make it drink. Yet, when the horse is really thirsty it drinks water with zeal. Therefore, the will to learn is very important in such cases. That said, learning is not a choice in this era of complex business realities where knowledge management efforts are directly linked to the return on investment (ROI) of organizations. Therefore, this underlying theme should be driven home to the workforce explicitly from the very beginning.

2) To avoid mistake

In the process of up-dating one's knowledge, it is also necessary to avoid committing mistakes while working. Sometimes, mistakes can turn out to be costly. For example, if your mistake results in financial loss to your employer, you may be held liable to make good the loss. Further, to correct such mistakes, you may spend twice or thrice the normal time you spend on such jobs. The mistake may also inconvenience the customer concerned. Your boss will not be happy either. On the whole, it could be a tiring and painful experience for all concerned.

3) To reduce dependency relations among employees

There is a tendency among many staff members to depend on a better-informed colleague for clarification of their doubts. Such a practice is good only up to a point. It should never become a regular practice. Everyone needs to strive to become self-confident and self-contained by improving knowledge, skills and creativity through reading and various other means.

What managements can do to improve Knowledge Management?

1) Ensure employee-friendly environment

An employee-friendly atmosphere is necessary for learning to take place smoothly. Therefore, managements should ensure that the tools for learning are easily accessible to the employees. Further, the process of learning should not result in any kind of disruption to an employee's family or social life. Wherever possible, the process of learning should also be incentivised.

2) Discard the redundant work processes

Banks must learn to differentiate between smart and hard ways of doing things. If they critically examine their work processes, they may observe many redundant steps, existing at various levels. If corrective steps are initiated, work efficiency and effectiveness can be automatically improved. Therefore, it is very important that a thorough time and work study of banking processes shall be initiated at the earliest. The old management styles and tools used should change with times, if need be. This will also make knowledge management all the more easy.

3) Reverse mentoring

Some organisations have adopted reverse mentoring, a method by which older executives and senior officials are guided or trained by the young employees on current trends in technology and social media. Reverse mentoring enables to bridge the knowledge gap of the elders. The redeeming feature is that it nurtures better culture and harmony in the workplace. This is a win-win situation for both.

4) Training and retraining

It was the author of *'Asian Drama'* Nobel Laureate Gunnar Myrdal who said in the 70s that expenditure for education is an investment for future. This is true in the case of a nation or organisation or even in the case of every individual. The banking organisations allowing the training system functioning in a half-hearted way is doing a disservice to their organisations.

The training system in the banks should be viewed as a university within the banks. A classical example is the Infosys Leadership Institute functioning in 337 acres in Mysore. Besides imparting training on banking, finance, management, soft skills and a host of related subjects, the banks can also impart *"How to live lessons"* to the staff members. After all, work or profession is one of the dimensions of the great enigma called LIFE. Officers with high level knowledge, extraordinary competence and aptitude for training should be selected for the post of faculty members.

How the employees can contribute to knowledge management?

1. Strengthening knowledge

Ignorance is darkness and knowledge always enlighten us. Knowledge dispels fear, enhances inner confidence and helps us to take quick and rational decisions. When all the employees update and improve their work-related knowledge on an ongoing basis the result will be hugely synergistic and this will eventually translate into sustained growth and progress of their organisations.

A banking job can be risky if an officer or for that matter, any employee holding a responsible position, does not have adequate knowledge of the guidelines, rules and regulations applicable to the job he/she is handling. To protect themselves from risks resulting from ignorance or misunderstanding, it is advisable that employees make it a habit to note down the gist of the important circulars issued by their Head Office or Zonal Office or RBI in a handy note book for periodic reference. If there have been several circulars on a particular subject, a special note can be made as cross reference for easy identification, as and when required. If some of them have become obsolete, this fact should be clearly recorded at the relevant places. Those who are computer-savvy can use their desk top or lap top in place of the note book for taking the steps suggested above. These little efforts may be very helpful in times of emergency.

2. Improve reading habit

Reading is very important for self-growth and development. It not only enhances one's knowledge and communication ability but also refines one's mental make-up in general. A promotion with an exotic designation does not automatically instil confidence, higher order leadership qualities, knowledge and skill in an Individual overnight. Competencies have to developed through extensive reading of books and journals related to banking, economics, finance, business and also those dealing with matters of general interest. Sharing personal experiences of seniors and peers are also a rich source of inputs for self-development. One should try to tap all these sources, whenever possible. It is not enough that one becomes a well-informed and efficient officer or subordinate employee; it is equally necessary that one becomes a well-rounded human being, possessing endearing personal qualities like love, empathy, compassion, forgiveness, brotherhood etc. One must also eschew the negative qualities like ego, arrogance, jealousy etc. The positive qualities will always stand one in good stead.

Many people cite lack of time as the reason for not being able to read. This is a fallacy. The real reason lies elsewhere. Perhaps, such people do not accord high priority to self-development or they may think, after working so hard at office, they are entitled to recreation and entertainment. Surely, they are. But, should recreation and entertainment take up so much time that one finds little time thereafter for productive activities like reading which are going to shape one's life and career in the days ahead? With proper prioritization and time management, it would be possible for anyone to do enough things needed to be done, day after day.

3. Preparing snapshots

Preparing snapshots of information on banking concepts and related topics is one of the best ways to enhance and improve your knowledge. If an officer/employee of a bank starts preparing such snapshots on various topics from the beginning of his career, over a period of time, he can have a fascinating goldmine of information at his disposal. The snapshots can be updated from time to time and profitably used at work. Further, it will be enormously helpful at the time when you prepare for promotional test/interview from one grade/cadre to another. Presented in bullet form, they look brief, crystal-clear and easily understandable. For a clearer idea about 'snapshots', a few illustrative ones are given below.

DUE DILIGENCE

- Due diligence refers to the care a reasonable person should take before entering into an agreement or a transaction with another party. In the financial sense, 'due diligence' refers to the process by which a bank or financial institution checks the identity, background and financial aspects of potential and existing customers. Due diligence includes checking on the borrower's address, pre-approval inspections of the borrower's workplace, verification of KYC documents, PAN number, verification of title to the property offered as security, interviewing the borrower, his competitors, suppliers, customers, employees etc.
- A comprehensive due diligence can also include reviews of technology used by the borrower, planned capital expenditure, obligations to outsiders, credit reports from other bankers, the internal management control and information system, industrial relations, employee compensation and benefits and environmental audit. Many loans can be prevented from becoming bad by ensuring proper due diligence before and after sanction.

ORGANIC GROWTH

- When business is grown by a unit using its own resources it is called organic growth. It is expansion from within as a result of a company developing new products and improving its market share by using its available core competencies.

PARKINSON'S LAW

- The above law named after its creator, Northcote Parkinson states thus, "Work expands to fill the time available for its completion". As a result of this, employees generally feel overworked irrespective of the workload. The greater the number of employees, the larger is the difficulty to co-ordinate.

- A large bureaucracy will generate enough internal work to keep itself 'busy' and so justify its continued existence without commensurate output. The situation generates more staff shortage, though the base workload remains the same.

REPO RATES

- The repo (repurchase) rate is simply the annualized interest rate at which banks borrow money from the Reserve Bank of India (RBI) over a short term. This rate is now used as a benchmark for interest on all retail loans.

- A reduction in the repo rate helps banks to get money at a cheaper rate. RBI expects the banks in turn to reduce interest rates while lending.

- Reverse Repo rate is the rate at which Reserve Bank of India borrows money from commercial banks within the country.

- Both the Repo rates are important monetary instruments used by RBI to increase or decrease money supply in the economy as warranted by the prevailing circumstances,

WILLFUL DEFAULTER

- A wilful defaulter is a borrower who defaults on his loan repayment obligation despite having the capacity to repay. He normally does not utilize the funds for the purpose for which they were raised and diverts them discreetly for some other purpose/s.

- While defaulting, the borrower may try to dispose of fixed assets including immovable property given as security without the bank's knowledge.

- If the borrower is declared wilful defaulter by a bank, it is difficult for him to access funds from any other source in the market.

WINDOW DRESSING AND FALSIFYING DATA

- Usually, branches prepare their balance sheet with cautious restraint. However, sometimes, they prepare it in such a way as to make their financial position at the end of the year look better than it really is. The 'dressing up" is done so deceptively so that it does not catch the eye immediately. The aforesaid practice is referred to as "Window dressing".

- In order to draw realistic conclusions from a window-dressed balance sheet, other documents such as schedules, notes and auditor's report are also to be scrutinized carefully.

The significant advantage of preparing snapshots is that you can easily memorize them and retrieve them quickly when needed. You can gainfully adopt this methodology with regard to useful information received in respect of any topic from time to time through circulars or any other source. Overtime, you will discover this hobby, a joyful experience.

4. Contributing to rationalisation of work processes etc

Employees are expected to be active participants in the overall functioning of an organization. In that capacity, they must do their best to contribute to the progress of the organization in whichever way they can. For example, being in close contact with the work processes followed in a bank, they could try to explore ways to work faster and smarter by cutting down the number of layers, process times etc. and thus, enhance customer satisfaction. Such active participation by employees also aids the process of knowledge and skill management.

5. Beware of atrophy

Technology is a ubiquitous phenomenon and it touches every conceivable sphere of human lives. It is supposed to make the living easier than it was. Artificial intelligence and machine learning have arrived in a very big way. We know that a technology is a double-edged sword. For example, the introduction of chat GPT is likely to reduce the thinking capability of the human being, which may lead to gradual atrophy of human mind - a dangerous situation indeed. Atrophy is the gradual decline of muscles because of the decreased activity and degeneration of cells.

The human mind should be used in the way in which it was conceived or designed by the nature. The reality manifested in the nature's scheme of things, no doubt, is the ultimate truth. As Luther Burbank has rightly put it, "There is no truth except the truth we discover in nature." Reading, writing, speaking and listening are all the fundamental way of acquiring and enhancing the knowledge and this process has been followed for generations. Any effort which hampers the innate development of the basic human learning functions in the name of enhancing comfort and luxury may lead to far reaching consequence for human lives. Therefore, it is prudent that all employees shall foster their cognitive learning process in their own interest.

Knowledge is power. It widens our mental horizon to do our jobs better and opens up the door of opportunities and creativity. Knowledge helps to earn us wealth, wisdom, success and respect in society. It also helps one to be a complete individual and a responsible and socially conscious citizen. When there are so many benefits to be had by acquiring knowledge, it will be foolish of anyone to neglect the need to acquire knowledge.

As I have mentioned above that knowledge is essential to gain wisdom, it is only appropriate that I discuss the difference between the concepts of "knowledge" and "wisdom" before concluding the chapter. Knowledge and wisdom do not mean the same thing. In fact, knowledge is one of the prerequisites for gaining wisdom; the others being experience and good judgment. Perhaps, the following light-hearted quotation of Brian O'Driscollbeautifully captures the essence of the distinction. He *said, "Knowledge is knowing that a tomato is a fruit. Wisdom is knowing not to put it in a fruit salad."*

While knowledge is acquired in different ways like education, observation, reading, listening to others etc, experience comes through application of the acquired knowledge in real life. Last but not the least, to be wise, one needs to have good judgment which comes from instinct, learning, experience, analytical skills, lack of bias, ethics etc. Good judgment enables us to distinguish between right and wrong, good and bad, moral and immoral, true and false and so on.

CHAPTER 7

Time Management : Some Useful Tips

"It's not enough to be busy, so are the ants. The question is what are we busy about?"
-Henry David Thoreau

"Try to imagine a life without time keeping. Birds are not late. A dog does not check its watch. Deer do not fret over passing birthdays. Man alone measures time... because of this, man alone suffers... a fear that no other creature endures. A fear of time running out."
-Mitch Albom, The Time Keeper

Demystifying time management

Time management is a misnomer and a figment imagination of man. In the linear universe there is no time. Yet for all practical purposes, 'time' remains as the standard yardstick for quantifying our activities and movements. Time is only a dimension of space-time which does not move. Down the ages, human beings have tried different ways to measure time. From time immemorial, across the world, the crowing of the rooster has been taken to mean its good morning call. Human beings have also relied on the length of the shadows cast by tall mountains or even trees to mark the passage of time.

The Earth and other planets in the solar system, the stars and billions of galaxies in the cosmic system stay or rotate in their orbits with hardly any variation in their trajectories. The Earth endlessly revolves around the Sun in its age-old trajectory which in turn paves way for the back-to-back change of seasons in our planet with amazing punctuality. This never-ending cosmic drama that has gone on unfolding before humanity with relentless regularity for millions of years tells us a very important truth about Nature that it is ever prompt, punctual, silent and disciplined. It never tires nor postpones things for a later date. Perhaps, Mother Nature through the template of regularity, punctuality and reliability followed by it is sending out an important message to us mortals, inhabiting in one of her most glorious creations, the Earth and the message is: "Time is precious, do not waste it. Use it wisely by proper planning and priority-driven time management." But how many of us pay heed to this message?

In a way we all may be adequately blessed with the gift of money, muscle and mind but the least thing we have is time. So, all we have to think and decide is what to do with the time of 24 hours given to us. Making allowance for the time spent on sleeping, we might have about 16 waking hours to work with every day, which is sufficient for anyone to do justice to all the tasks that he or she has to carry out in a day. Yet we feel that the time available is insufficient to complete our tasks, thanks to the inadequate Time Management skills we possess. According to Stephen Covey the essence of time management can be captured in a single phrase: *"Organise and execute around priorities."* Hence, allotting the right amount of time for each task and deciding the sequence of executing the tasks based on the importance of each is very crucial in Time Management. The important steps in effective Time Management are: Meticulous planning, setting goals and objectives, prioritization of tasks based on their importance, allotting the right amount of time to each job, setting deadlines for each task and delegating responsibilities.

How to improve your time management skills?

Let's now examine the various ways of improving our time management skills.

1. Accepting responsibility

The first step towards effective Time Management is accepting responsibility for the tasks entrusted to us combined with the determination to work towards the successful completion of each of them. In the organizational context, it would mean that before an employee is hired, he should be given a clear idea as to what his responsibilities are, the way each task is to be performed, the minimum required level of performance and who the employee should be reporting to. The world-renowned psychologist Scott Peck has succinctly summed up the importance of responsibility in the following words: "We can't solve life's problems except by solving them."

2. *Plan meticulously*

Planning is very important in the management process. It enables you to have a proper road map before you start work on the various tasks awaiting you. It is always good to start the day with a "To do" list containing the details of the tasks to be executed based on the planning exercise. The plan must be flexible, not rigid.

3. *Prioritise*

As already mentioned, the core of time management is executing work around priorities. Just imagine a situation where, on reaching office, you decide that you are going to attend to each pending letter in your tray in the order they are kept. If you work this way, it is quite possible that in the evening, you might find a number of letters marked "Very urgent" or "Urgent" still not attended, even though quite a few less important or unimportant ones are attended. This kind of working may result in lot of quantity but in terms of outcomes, it is the least productive. We should therefore always embrace the time-tested principle of 'First Things First' or prioritizing and scheduling our tasks for the day in the order of their importance while leaving room for accommodating minor readjustments. Accordingly, the 'To do' list can be drawn up in the form of an ABC list where A stands for the most important tasks execution of which yields the highest value. These tasks are usually not delegable. B stands for the less important tasks which are partly delegable and C stands for the least important tasks like telephoning, filing, correspondence and other sundry routine work. For preparing the ABC list, we can also make profitable use of the Pareto principle (or the 80:20 rule), a helpful concept with wide applications. What it basically says is that 80 per cent of the output from a given situation or system is determined by 20 per cent of the input. It can be used not just in management but also in various other areas including our private lives. Some practical examples of the principle are given below.

- 80% of your sales is to 20% of your clients.
- 80% of your profits come from 20% of your products.
- You wear 20% of your clothes 80% of the time.
- 20 % of your products generate 80% of your sales.

Now let us take the statement appearing against the last bullet point above and consider its practical application. Let's say you are head of the Complaints section in a company and the higher management has asked you to take necessary steps in the light of the said statement. Normally, as head of the Complaints section, the best way for you to use it would be this: On the basis of the data, you know that 80% of your sales are generated by 20% of your products. You should now try to identify the products that make up the 20% and place all the complaints related to them in the A section of your list (Most important). Rest of the complaints can come under 'B' or 'C" as the case may be. By using the Pareto principle while preparing the ABC list, we can ensure that time spent on various activities is commensurate with the value they bring to the organization.

4. Procrastination

Procrastination or postponing things which signifies the tendency of indecision, is said to be the biggest thief of time. By sitting over a matter, no one can remain relaxed or happy for long. Sooner or later, the matter will have to be decided. But, by then the delay might give rise to various complications including loss in money terms. Hence, one should make it a point to shun avoidance behaviour, eschew the habit of postponing and utilise the time at our disposal effectively.

5. Attending promptly to urgent and important matters

An urgent work is that which is lying just in front of you and which seeks your immediate action. If important things are not done promptly, you will always live in urgency crisis. In most cases, a matter may not be urgent when it is received. But, when it is not addressed within a reasonable time due to laziness or indifference, it naturally becomes urgent or very urgent or most urgent depending on how much time it remained unattended. Habitual laziness or indifference may land one in a perennial crisis-ridden state resulting in extreme work-related stress. The best way to avoid this is to attend the prioritised work unfailingly within a reasonable period of time.

6. Delegate

Many people avoid delegating work to their subordinates for different reasons. Some do not do it out of fear of undermining their own importance and indispensability. There are also those who avoid delegation because they find it cumbersome as it involves spending time on explaining the job concerned to another person, clarifying his doubts and doing the necessary handholding, at least in the initial stages. There is also another category of people who believe that they alone can do a perfect job and who do not trust the abilities of others. The result is that such people try to do everything themselves which often leads to delays resulting in complaints, quality issues etc. After all, there is a limit to what one man can do all by himself.

Avoiding delegation is not a sensible approach to manpower management. Every organization should ensure grooming people for the next level so that as and when a vacancy arises at any level due to retirement or otherwise, there is always someone available to fill the breach. Delegation is a necessary part of such grooming and facilitates succession planning and management.

7. *Avoid cluttering*

Sometimes, you may find your table getting more and more cluttered with each passing day. At such times, you should first go through each item and keep them in separate holders according to their priority and go about clearing them regularly and meticulously. Unless the aforesaid is done, the clutter will grow and so will your stress which will take its toll on your health.

8. *Avoid the 'No time' excuse*

Many people cite paucity of time as the reason for their failure to do one job or the other. This reactive habit gradually becomes an inseparable part of their nature and they themselves start believing that the 'No time' explanation is not an excuse but the truth. In fact, with proper planning and prioritization, the number of waking hours everyone gets is sufficient to attend to the tasks awaiting him or her in a day.

9. *Maintain good health*

Researchers from RAND Corporation in California recently conducted a study on how Americans spend their waking hours. The study revealed that all the respondents had more leisure time than they thought they did but few of them were using even a portion of that free time for physical activity. These respondents defined leisure time as involving activities that were not in some way required or compulsory. The time devoted for exercising, socialising, relaxing, playing, watching TV, chatting with friends, travelling for pleasure or otherwise not working constituted their leisure time. The findings suggest that if people adjusted their schedules and turned off their TV, phone or computer, most of them would have plenty of time to work out. This is indicative of the negative impact of overuse of the above gadgets. People must understand that exercise and other physical activities, good eating habits, positive thinking etc. go a long way in ensuring good health. Needless to add, lack of good health can weaken our will power, which will adversely impact our decision-making ability and Time Management skills.

10. Learn to say "no" when required

You may come across situations where your boss or a colleague may try to dump his work on you as a matter of habit. There is nothing wrong in obliging such people once in a while for genuine reasons if it is not inconvenient to you. However, where the motive behind such requests is to exploit your generosity or where saying 'Yes' to them could impact your well-being or adversely affect the quality of work actually assigned to you, it may be time to politely say 'No' to such requests. Dissent should not be viewed as disloyalty or insubordination, for good reasons. It is not wise to treat all of our critics as our enemies. The boss is human and so he can also go wrong, at times. We live in a society where a well-entrenched habit of pleasing the authority figures has become our second nature.

In such situations, it is always desirable that the reasons for your inability to oblige is clearly explained to the other side so as not to give room for any misunderstanding. It will bring you inward freedom and it can even save a career or life. As a matter of fact, the person who says 'No' sensibly is the one who will be respected most in our culture in the long run. As Norman Vincent Peale said, "Most of us would rather be ruined by praise than saved by criticism."

11. Avoid needless use of telephone/mobile phones

Telephone/Mobile phones are the most ubiquitous communication tools available today. They are used for a number of purposes, the main ones being: communication, education, e-banking and finance, photo and video shoots, entertainment, navigation, notes and reminders, online orders, bookings and payments etc. Telephones/mobile phones are quite indispensable for all irrespective of the age or profession of the people, but we should not waste our time on unproductive and frivolous pursuits.

12. Avoid too much multi-tasking

Some of us of the view that multitasking helps us to complete more than one task in a shorter period of time and thus, makes us more efficient. Multi-tasking makes it difficult for us to attend to any task with focused attention. This means that when you do and redo more things simultaneously, there can be more room for errors of omission and commission. Even if you take extra time, multi-tasking may actually turn out to be a wasteful way of doing things. Hence, multi-tasking should be resorted to only when there are proven benefits to be had by engaging in it.

Before finalising our discussion on Time management, I cannot think of a better way than by quoting the lines of ***Charles Buxton,*** which capture the very essence of the whole discussion: ***"You will never find time for anything. If you want time, you must make it."***

CHAPTER 8

Maintaining Good Health And Managing Stress : Understanding The Wellness Code

"BEWARE OF THE BARRENNES OF BUSY LIFE."
- SOCRATES

"Health is the greatest gift, contentment is the greatest wealth."
- Dhammapada

This essay broadly deals with two important aspects of life which are closely inter-related: maintaining good health and managing stress. As banks are service-oriented organisations, good health is indispensable for enhancing the job-related competencies of an employee. Intermittent or prolonged state of ill-health is likely to affect his performance adversely. For example, ill-health in any form could seriously interfere with his decision-making ability or unpleasantly affect the quality of his interactions with the clients, the stakeholders and the general public.

At the risk of stating a truism, I must emphasize that good health is undoubtedly the most important possession in life without which no one can enjoy the gift of living a full life. Paradoxically, there also exists the hard reality of sickness merchants (read, pharma companies and overcharging hospitals) who profit from human sickness. In the words of Aldous Huxley, "*Medical science has made such tremendous progress that there is hardly a healthy human left.*" Hence, for all practical purposes, living by the old adage, 'Prevention is better than cure' is the best way to maintain good health.'

In this chapter we focus further on two aspects of health, one relating to four key functions of maintaining health such as Breathing, Eating & Exercising, Sleeping and Thinking and another relating to the goal of achieving Physical, Mental or Psychological, Emotional and Spiritual health, which are holistic and mutually reinforcing phenomena.

HOW TO LIVE HEALTHY?

Every human being is entitled to a disease-free life. But, such a life does not happen automatically. One has to work for it. For this, we have to first go back to the basics and start scrupulously following some universally acknowledged best practices in our breathing, eating, exercising, sleeping and thinking habits. We can remember these fundamental life-sustaining human functions by way of an acronym, BEST (B- Breathing, E-Eating & Exercising, S-Sleeping and T-Thinking). By regularly and continuously finetuning the BEST as our preventive health care regimen, we can avoid, if not minimise visits to a doctor to a great extent. Let's now examine the matter in greater detail.

Breathing

Breathing the right way has a number of beneficial effects on our physical, mental and emotional health. Some of these are as follows:

a) Helps oxygenation of the body.
b) Clears the lungs and purifies the blood.
c) Tones up the nervous system.
d) Helps to keep blood pressure normal.
e) Helps to get rid of the accumulated carbon-dioxide.
f) Reduces tension.
g) Improves immunity, concentration and vision.
h) Prevents stiffening of muscles and joints, headache and backache.
i) Ensures good digestion and better sleep.
j) Mitigates degenerative diseases.
j) Prevents constipation, indigestion and acidity.

The right way to breathe is to breathe deeply from our abdomen and through the nose while keeping the spine straight without straining. We should start inhale through the left nostril for 4 seconds, hold the breath for 12 seconds and then slowly exhale for 8 seconds. Repeat the process through right nostril. You can slightly reduce or increase the counts depending upon your lung capacity. The best way to ensure breathing right is to learn *Pranayama* from a master and practise it for at least 10-15 minutes in the morning and the evening on a daily basis.

This regular practice of Pranayama gradually will positively influence our normal breathing too.

Metaphorically, the daily practice of *Pranayama* is to the mind what the daily removal of dirt is to a house. *Pranayama* is essentially a cleansing process. However, those suffering from lung-related problems should seek a doctor's advice before they start practising P*ranayama.*

Eating

As the age-old saying goes, "You are what you eat." Overeating causes gastric heaviness in the stomach, sleeplessness, acidity, chronic indigestion and constipation. As a result, our entire body, mind and emotions turn dull and toxic. Frequent indigestion and constipation upset correct rhythm of breathing, trigger wrong kind of thoughts and spoil sleep. Such a situation may adversely affect our day-to-day decision-making ability. Overeating of food items also causes damage to the cell membranes and tissues and depletes vitamins in the body. Calorie-rich foods lead to fat deposits which may result in weight gain, diabetes and clogging up of arteries. Too much intake of salt can lead to high blood pressure. Balanced and nutritious food is the key to good health. In fact, one needs very less food to lead a healthy life. Therefore, both wrong eating and overeating should be avoided. Vegetarian food is always safer for our bodies. Therefore, it is better to reduce if not avoid, non-vegetarian food.

Saliva produced when food is chewed well and this helps digestion and prevents constipation, acidity and flatulence. Drinking eight glasses of water every day is ideal. Eating water content fruits like guava, apple, watermelon etc is also good for keeping away indigestion. Besides all these, adequate rest by way of occasional fasting, is essential to our overworked digestive organs.

Exercise

Exercise and yoga can help people across all age groups to maintain their fitness. Exercise strengthens our muscular, hormonal and nervous systems and helps us to manage our weight, improves digestive system and enhances general well-being.

Posture of an individual (in sitting, standing and lying positions) has much to do with the alignment of spine and its adjoining bone structures. Bad posture for long hours causes wear and tear of tissues leading to osteoarthritis; it also disrupts the load-bearing balance of our joints. Too much of over-stretching may cause irretrievable damage to the bones. Therefore, prior medical advice is desirable before attempting exercises involving overstretching. Similarly, a person with a weak heart should not do heavy exercises, as this may invite cardiac arrest. A word of caution here. Do not reduce exercise to a competition with someone. Do it at your own pace lest it should become counterproductive to your health.

Brisk walking for about an hour daily and exposure to sunlight for a minimum of 10 minutes a day is highly recommended. Such exposure helps us to absorb the radiant energy emanating from the sun. It can also destroy harmful microbes in our bodies. However, over-exposure to sunlight should be avoided. Ideally, physical exercises and yoga should be done under the guidance of a skilled trainer.

Sleeping

Adequate sleep is very essential for good health. Causes of sleeplessness can be physical or mental or both. Sleeplessness is normally a symptom of poor general health. Sleeplessness induces bodily ailments and quickens wear and tear of our body.

It will be ideal to take a bath in the evening, have dinner preferably between 7.30 and 8 p.m. and go to sleep between 9.30 and 10 p.m. A minimum of 6-8 hrs sleep is needed by a normal human being. Heavy intake of food and water before sleep should be avoided. Usage of computer, laptop, mobile phone etc. should be stopped at least one or two hours before sleeping time as the research reveals, light emitted from the screens of these devices misleads our brain into believing night to be day, which hinders the production of Melatonin hormone in our body. As a result, we do not get good sleep. You may also try reading a book before going to bed as this can often stimulate sleep. The doctors suggest avoiding stimulants like nicotine, caffeine and alcohol if one is looking for sound sleep. Also, you can try the simple distractive technique of counting from 1 to 50, lying on the bed. If need be, repeat this counting till you fall asleep.

Observe your Thoughts

Day in and day out, many of us witness the procession of foreboding feelings within that something unpleasant or dangerous is going to happen. In other words, more often we are captivated and victimised by such imaginary thoughts. They trigger stress within us and as a result, our body and mind become toxic. Our thoughts can be voluntary and involuntary. Voluntary thoughts are generated consciously. Involuntary thoughts which spring from our subconscious thoughts are mostly negative. Involuntary thoughts can be resisted by choosing positive thoughts or engaging in some useful hobbies/ productive activities. Recent research studies reveal that a human being entertains an average 60,000 thoughts every day and 90% of them are repeated or negative thoughts.

As Swami Vivekananda said once, "We are what our thoughts have made us; so take care about what you think. Words are secondary. Thoughts live; they travel far." It has been further said that there is nothing in this world that can trouble us more than our own thoughts. We must therefore observe our way of thinking occasionally and unlearn faulty habits. Alongside, also learn to restrain ego and avoid judging everything instantly. Cheerful thoughts are the best antidote for illness. Practise forgiveness and make life simple and less cumbersome. Right living will take care of the future in its own way.

The four-fold goals

Now let us discuss the four-fold goals of achieving Physical, Mental or Psychological, Emotional and Spiritual health to bring about a balanced and integrated development of the personality of an individual.

Physical health

Physical health basically refers to the condition of our physical body and how it works. It should be our aim to keep our bodies active and disease-free through exercise and a balanced diet. Again, keeping the body idle is akin to keeping one's car in the shed without using it. In both cases, the respective physical bodies are bound to deteriorate faster. Atrophy (losing flesh, muscle and strength due to inadequacy of blood) will set in.

Mental or Psychological health

Mental or psychological health refers to balancing the emotions, thoughts and behaviour of a person and in case of imbalance among the three, various issues are likely to arise. It has been said that body is mind in action. Body is the gross manifestation and mind is the finer manifestation. Mind is the epicentre of the thoughts and emotions. The spiralling thoughts and emotions surface as action and behaviour in the body. Therefore, we must empower our self by education - by reading and listening the scriptures and other good books regularly. One should also engage in hobbies like creative writing, singing, playing music and games etc. as such activities are effective antidotes to psychological disorders.

Emotional health

It refers to the awareness and understanding a person has about his/her emotions and his ability to cope with changes and uncertainties. Emotions have immense power. Negative emotions like anger, fear and worry unleash harmful chemicals and damage the nerves. The toxic hormones inside the body in turn breed numerous physical, emotional and psycho-somatic complications. On the other hand, many positive emotions have beneficial effects on our overall health.

Spiritual health

Spiritual health enables one to connect to a higher purpose in life. This helps one to lead a full life and also find hope and comfort even at the most trying times. The higher purpose could be connecting to God or serving the poor or social service or any other similar activity. Regular meditation, occasional retreat into solitude and communion with Nature etc. are some of the other ways recommended for spiritual health.

If you make investment in the aforesaid goals, it will pave the way for ensuring good health and improve your personal growth. This will hugely improve the productivity of your organisation. Needless to say, as a prelude to all success, discipline of the body, mind and spirit is highly essential.

MANAGING STRESS

What is stress?

Stress does not lie in the events or disturbances that happen outside. They lie in our own response to what happens outside. When we are under stress, the sympathetic branch of our autonomous nervous system is aroused and as a result, massive physical, emotional and behavioural changes take place in us. Hypothalamus activates the pituitary gland, causing release of a rush of stress hormones including adrenaline and cortisol. These hormones prepare our bodies to meet the emergency before us. Our muscles start tightening, our hearts start pounding faster and we start getting breathless and so on. Adrenaline is a powerful stimulant important for our survival response. When adrenaline is released, the body performs beyond its normal capacity. Cortisol on the other hand has many functions but it mainly helps our body to respond to stress by increasing our blood sugar level which in turn boosts our energy levels.

UNDERSTANDING STRESS AND HOW IT AFFECTS YOU

Symptoms indicative of stress are physical, mental and emotional. Some of the *Physical Symptoms* manifested are: palpitations, rapid/shallow breathing, persistent head-aches, indigestion, constipation or diarrhoea, viral infections, frequent urination, skin problems, irregularity in the menstrual cycle etc. *Behavioral Symptoms* include faulty planning, poor concentration, forgetfulness, nervousness, biting of nails, phobic fears, sleeplessness, loss of libido etc. *Emotional Symptoms* manifested are fear, anxiety, loss of confidence, irritability etc.

Stress can’t be avoided entirely. While positive stress can motivate us and strengthen our performance, negative stress will diminish our enthusiasm and quality of life. By reducing stress, our precious energy can be used in more positive ways.

How to manage stress?

Understand the basic truth that life is not easy. When you truly internalize that life is not easy, eventually you will discover life is easy. In the same vein, we must acknowledge that stress is integral to our lives and it cannot be wished away. There are ways to manage stress and mitigate its side effects. Some of them are discussed in the following lines.

1. Meditation

The logic of meditation centres on disciplining and focusing of our thoughts. It helps us to achieve great feats in life. Meditation promotes all-round expansion and development of an individual. When our sensuous, fearful and depressed thoughts are renounced intelligently we can live in a state of enduring joy.

Meditation awakens the body, mind and soul. Regular and intense meditation brings enormous positive benefits all through the day. Reserve a separate space or room in your house for this purpose and make yourself free from distractions. If you practise Relaxation, *Pranayama* and Meditation (RPM) mindfully and regularly, you can reduce, if not altogether avoid the not-so-happy experience of visiting doctors and consuming costly medicines. To be mindful means to feel fully present in the here-and now-situation, totally ignoring the unpleasant experiences of the past and the benumbing anxieties of the future.

2. Build Relationships

Stephen Covey says, "Our greatest pain and greatest pleasure come from our relationship with others." Ensure that no one disturbs your mind without your permission. Be simple in your thoughts, manner and style of doing things and interact with people positively and honestly. Words uttered can create a hell or a heaven. Therefore, exercise care while using words. This will protect you and create peace within.

3. Our fearful thoughts

Our unending fearful thoughts and our indifference to leading a simple life aggravate stress. We continuously think of the past and future, ignoring the present. Present is precious and it is right in front of us. If we think and act rightly in the present, we can ensure a peaceful and happy future. By worrying about the past and being anxious about the future, we can only make our present flawed and complicated. Always choose to be happy. Voltaire said, "I have to chosen to be happy because it is good for my health."

4. Humour/Smile

Humour releases tension and reduces stress. Laughter helps to bring down our blood pressure level. It provides relaxation to our muscles, drives away worries and enhances energy level. Practise smiling as it is infectious. It costs nothing and fits into all occasions. Say simple words like *'sorry'* or *'thank you'* frequently in your conversation with others. Such words can narrow the distance between people and take the relationship and intimacy between them to a new level.

5. Anger

Our body is a mysterious chemical factory functioning with its various systems. For example, our endocrine system is responsible for unleashing a range of emotions within us like anger, fear, anxiety, depression etc. While all of these are equally harmful to our health, anger specifically is a dreadful emotion which can cause huge upheavals in our thoughts and actions, affecting not only us but also those around us. So, when your anger crosses all limits, it may perhaps be time to go for a medical check-up and consult your doctor.

Strategies for Controlling Anger

The best antidote to anger is to remain silent, no matter how others behave. Anger poisons the whole bodily system. When angry thoughts shoot slowly, try to control them at the sprouting stage itself. Maintain silence for a moment; listen and grasp the words of the speaker carefully. When anger surges, close your eyes with your palms, take a deep breath and expel it slowly. You will feel that carbon dioxide is expelled from your lungs, fresh air is infused into your respiratory system and your cells are energised. Calm prevails.

Another approach is to shift your thoughts consciously to some unrelated ideas or events or count from 1 to 10. Or else, leave the scene for a while wilfully. Care should be taken to modulate and soften your voice and refine your body language while speaking on such occasions.

Anger begets anger. Sometimes, it may not be possible to avoid anger completely. So instead of suppressing anger and frustrations completely, they can be articulated in a gentle and moderate way without hurting the other side. Anyhow, try to find out the cause of your anger and find a solution through rational thinking.

6. Fitness Exercise

Exercise helps to improve oxygenation and blood circulation. It strengthens muscles, activates the nervous system and ensures prolonged general health. It is an effective antidote for the various diseases linked to our modern sedentary lifestyles. As we age, our nerves, muscles and skeletal systems gradually degenerate and may turn dysfunctional. Bad posture causes wear and tear of tissues. A half-an-hour to one hour brisk walking every day is always good for health. The adrenaline and cortisol levels are effectively kept in check by regular exercise.

7. Relaxation Exercise - CALM

You can mentally instruct your head, torso (trunk of our body), hands and legs to relax for five to ten seconds each; CALM stands for Chest, Arms, Legs and Mouth (for head). You can imaginatively scan muscle tension of the neck, shoulders, chest, stomach, thighs, calf muscles, toes and also upper and lower arms and instruct them individually to be 'calm' and 'relaxed.' When your thoughts massage your body step-by-step, you'll feel like imaginary waves sweeping off the body tensions. Repeat this process for 2–3 minutes. Optionally, you can also practise the progressive relaxation technique in which skeletal muscles beginning with the feet upwards are tensed and relaxed alternately, progressing from one muscle group to another.

8. Lead a simple life and count your blessings

Simple living is always the key to robust health, inner peace and happiness. Possessing less and leading a debt-free life brings more freedom and contentment. Enjoying material possessions may give pleasure and excitement initially but it eventually ends up in suffering.

How to practise simplicity?

Right thinking and simple life are complementary to each other. Simplicity must be initiated from our homes. One should start by de-cluttering the home environment by getting rid of disused old clothes, unused books, old toys, unused utensils etc. At home or office, everything should be arranged and kept in the appropriate place. When required, you should also be able to quickly retrieve them.

Before you spend, always differentiate between needs and wants. A need is a necessity e.g. food, water, clothes and so on which are essential for survival. Want is a choice and it is often shaped by the expectation of others. Never waste money celebrating family events like marriage and other festivals with borrowed money. Whatever challenges one may face in life, never turn your back on values like love, trust, intimacy, compassion, patience etc. which ensure family harmony and social unity. When you shun vanity and modern consumerism, you will feel that life is simple, peaceful and harmonious. As Elise Boulding says, "*The consumption society has made us feel that happiness lies in having things, and has failed to teach us the happiness of not having things.*"

Count your blessings

Take a glass half-filled with water. We can interpret the same situation in different ways. While someone may complain that the glass is half empty, another may say it is half full, 'so let me enjoy what is available'. A third one may count it as God's blessing and thank Him for it. In any challenging situation, life gives you new opportunities; seize them. Ability to see positives in the midst of negative situation can defuse stress instantly.

9. Family first, Time-Outs and Solitude

Normally, family is where your heart is. It is a place where you enjoy your ultimate freedom. Find time to enjoy life with family and children. Thrive and succeed first in your family. All your winning streaks outside put together cannot match a happy and healthy family life in terms of satisfaction. Make regular visits to places of interest, call on relatives and strengthen relations. Enjoy reflecting on the mysteries of Nature in moments of solitude. It will help you to recharge psychologically and emotionally.

10. Time Management

Time is the greatest asset. People consider time as an entitlement and waste it lavishly. We always complain there is no time to do our work and procrastinate callously. Everyone's life ends with the expiry of the allotted time on this planet. Simple and eternal truths like this rarely engage our attention. One must be conscious of them and spend time wisely. *(Read also 'Time Management' Chapter 7).*

I am sure, if you make investment in the aforesaid goals and follow the suggested tips of stress management, it will be a highly rewarding experience in your life and in turn, it will hugely improve the productivity of your organisation. I wish you all good luck and hope that you will finally achieve what you set out to achieve. But remember that good health and a stress-free life are not achieved in a jiffy. It takes a steely resolve, immense will power, self-denial and months of relentless practice before one achieves the two objectives mentioned above. It's quite possible that you might not see any tangible benefits accruing from your efforts initially. This might tempt you to shed all the self-imposed discipline and go back to your unhealthy ways. You may even start rationalising this regression by telling yourself that with all the stress that you are subject to, you are entitled to indulge yourself in whatever manner you choose. These are the moments to beware of and make sure that you bring all your determination, will power and capacity for self-denial into full play so that you stay the course. And for inspiration, you need not look further than the following words of the great Nelson Mandela: ***"Do not judge me by my successes, judge me by how many times I fell down and got back up again."***

CHAPTER 9

Personal Counselling: Equipping Your People To Navigate Life's Challenges With Confidence

'Give light and people will find the way.'
- Ella Baker

'Give a man a fish and you can feed him for a day;
teach him how to fish and you feed him for a lifetime.'
- Chinese proverb

WHAT IS COUNSELLING?

Counselling is a kind of conversation between a counsellor and his client (counsellee) during which the former tries to understand the deep-seated emotional problems faced by the latter and then proceeds to discuss with him (counsellee) how he can cope with them better. A counselling relationship is a relationship based on mutual trust, respect and empathetic understanding in which the client (counsellee) learns to discuss openly with the counsellor what worries and upsets him. During the process, the counsellor helps to bring out and show the counselee his hidden potential and resources so that the latter can improve his self-awareness and resolve his emotional problems himself, if necessary, by bringing about changes in his personality and behaviour. Where counselling helps resolution of the adjustment-related problems of the counselee while dealing with other people, the counsellor strengthens the counsellee's self-confidence to deal with his frustrations and inner conflicts and enables him to become a fully-functioned individual. From helping individuals to develop courage and confidence to showing them the way to take timely and correct decisions, the scope for using the tool of counselling is truly wide. The nature and content of counselling will be decided by the needs of the counsellee as assessed by the counsellor. However, counselling helps only those who are ready to help themselves.

Modern organisations are increasingly depending on professional counselling for improving interpersonal relationships of their employees and ensuring proper work-life balance in their lives. As all of us know, a banking job comes with a lot of risks and responsibilities which takes a heavy toll on the health of many banking personnel. During this writer's interactions with a good number of bank officers and executives over the years, what stood out was the widely prevailing sense of frustration among them with regard to the conditions in which they worked and the resulting adverse effects on their work-life balance. Not surprisingly, many of them suffered from psychosomatic problems. In the following pages, an attempt has been made to give an overview of the counselling process. It is hoped that the overview will serve as a useful introductory guide to the readers in understanding the nuances of counselling and possibly, using that knowledge to find solutions to some of their own problems as well as those faced by their friends, colleagues and subordinates, in both their private and working lives.

Goals of Counselling

Major goals of counselling are: facilitating behavioural change, enhancing coping skills and improving decision-making, relationships and personal effectiveness. All such goals mostly involve bringing about changes in one's behaviour and/or personality. The ***three stages*** of change are: self-exploration, understanding and action. For example, if you want to control your fear, first you have to ***explore*** the *what, why, when and how* aspects of your fear by repeatedly asking yourself the relevant questions. Such self-probing enables you to clearly ***understand*** your problem, which in turn helps you to find a solution for it and ***act*** accordingly.

QUALITIES OF A GOOD COUNSELLOR

1.Positive human qualities

A counsellor must possess positive human qualities like love, compassion, warmth, trust, genuineness and common sense. He should also have deep interest in and empathetic understanding of people. He must have emotional stability and objectivity and be approachable to clients. He should have sufficient knowledge about his domain and show good judgment skills while dealing with human problems. He should never sit in judgment over the conduct of the counsellee and force him to follow his views.

2. Listening and communication skills

Listening is the key to counselling. Most of the problems in life are triggered by the lack of listening. The counsellor listens to the client attentively and with unconditional positive regard, enters the frame of reference of the counsellee. That is to say, the counsellor temporarily begins to see himself in relation to the world around the client just as the latter would do. He also accepts the counsellee as he or she is, without any judgment. Apart from being a good listener, a counsellor must also be good at communication as he has to get the counsellee to open up without leaving out anything. For this, he has to be skilful, articulate, persuasive and also gentle to avoid the counselee getting offended.

3. Empathy

The words empathy and sympathy are extensively used in relation to interpersonal relations. Sympathy is sharing the feelings of concern for the sufferings of another person with that person and expressing compassion for him. It brings great relief to any sufferer when he receives sympathy. But, sympathy alone will not solve a sufferer's problem. Empathy, on the other hand, is imaginatively experiencing the experience of another person or in other words, putting yourself in the shoes of another. In effect, it is the act of entering the frame of reference of another person. When you empathize with your daughter after she has suffered a setback in her personal life, you are trying to accurately understand her feelings and also trying to mitigate her problem. And your communications also reflect that. In such moments, both of you are on the same wavelength. In sympathy, though you are emotionally involved with her sorrow, you may not understand her needs and position objectively.

Counselling is basically a process of listening empathetically. If the counsellor is trustworthy, the counsellee will speak about his personal problems to him candidly. He will undergo a kind of catharsis during the counselling process which will help him to recover from his accumulated distress. He will now feel more confident of solving his problems.

Carl Rogers, in his celebrated book, '*A way of Being*,' appreciates an individual for the way he normally appreciates sunset. No one can control the fascinating celestial spectacle of sunset. On seeing sunset, one cannot say, "*soften the orange a little on the right-hand corner, put a bit more purple along the base, and use a little more pink in the cloud color.*" One simply watches this cosmic wonder as it unfolds. It is in this spirit a counsellor should listen to a counselee in the moments of counselling. In other words, he should listen to the counsellee with unconditional positive regard and high esteem.

4. Respect

A counsellor must respect and accept the worth of the counsellee as he is. He must treat him as a person and feel convinced about his potential for personal growth. His freedom and right to make decisions must be recognized and respected.

5. Self-disclosure

When the counsellee opens up his heart to the counsellor, he may naturally like to know the latter intimately. In such cases, a good counsellor should not hesitate to disclose his personal details to the counsellee if it is absolutely necessary for the counselling process to proceed; of course, such personal details must be credible.

6. Patience

Counselling was never an easy task. Sometimes it may take months or even years to get the counsellee to open up and come out with the truth or to realise that he himself is responsible for something gone wrong in his life. In such cases, the counsellor should not throw up his hands and quit. Instead, he must patiently wait for the right time and opportunity to resume his conversations with the counsellee.

7. Reasoning and research skills

A counsellee's replies may not always be consistent. This makes arriving at the truth difficult for any counsellor. In such cases, the counsellor should try to use his reasoning skills and ask probing questions or even a single question in more than one way to get at the truth. All this will need to be done gently and persuasively without offending the counsellee. A counsellor should also be good at research so as to make full use of the experiential learning and data base available to him through his counselling sessions with people from diverse backgrounds.

8. Observational skills

To be a good counsellor, it is important to have good observational skills. This is because a counselee may sometimes be reluctant to give certain details concerning a problem or may give a distorted version of an event. The way the counselee speaks, his body language, the expression on his face etc. normally carries enough clues to indicate whether he is telling the truth or lying. An experienced counsellor should be able to read the clues and start a different line of enquiry to get at the truth.

THE COUNSELLING PROCESS

The counsellor should offer a pleasant atmosphere to the clients to freely air out their problems and concerns. The room selected for counselling should be comfortable, secured and well-ventilated with good lighting and without any kind of disturbance. The counsellor and the counsellee should sit face-to-face and have eye contact to the extent possible.

To begin with, the client may be hesitant to speak out honestly. In order to make him open up, the counsellor must display trustworthiness and establish empathic understanding with him. It is very important that he avoid being judgmental. He must help the client if he is confused or her words are not consistent. He should display enough patience and give the client time to complete what he has to say.

As the counselling progresses, the client may verbalize feelings, and shed tears. In counselling parlance, this is called discharging. Crying has deep therapeutic effect and it is an effective tension-releaser. Therefore, the counsellor shouldn't prevent it. When the situation settles, the counsellor can ask him to talk more about the problem.

Is Counselling an Advice-giving Process?

A counsellor is ordinarily not expected to give advice to the clients, although advice can be offered to them in some exceptional situations. But, in such cases, the counsellor must be clearly aware of the risks involved e.g. Suppose, a counsellor prescribes a solution to a problem and later on, it is found to be ineffective. Clearly, this can adversely affect the counsellor's credibility. Fundamentally, a counsellor's job is to help his client rediscover his potential and confidence and enable him to resolve his emotional problems himself. To do this, the counsellor has to first go deep down into the various motivational factors or causes behind the problem faced by his client and bring them to the latter's knowledge for finding a solution. If requested, the counsellor can explain to the client the various available options and their relative merits or demerits, leaving the final decision to the client. But, strictly speaking, it is not the job of the counsellor to talk about the solutions as the very purpose of counselling is to enable the patient to stand on his feet and take decisions for himself. As can be seen from the above, counselling is essentially a process of empowerment.

Banker as a counsellor

It is a truism to say that, a banker profoundly touches the lives of his customers. But, there is another equally important but less-discussed aspect to the profession of a banker: His leadership role vis-a-vis his team members. In any service organisation including a bank, people are the single most important asset. The mental and emotional aspects of employees' lives have a direct bearing on their work. And the reason for this is that many employees tend to carry their personal and family problems into their workplaces. It is easy to advise them to leave the baggage of such problems at home before starting for their workplace and *vice versa*. But, that is easier said than done. Amidst the increasing number and complexity of problems, life is getting over-complicated by the day and peace is becoming more and more elusive. It has got worse in recent times due to the Covid-19 pandemic experience, the recurring economic downturns, the frequent environmental disasters and deeply disturbing social distress et al. Needless to say, in such a situation, an employee, be he an office assistant or a CEO, is faced with multifarious challenges in varying degrees both in his private and working lives. Coping up with these problems can often be a Herculean task for anyone. No wonder that stress-induced illnesses like perennial anxiety, depression, manic-depressive psychosis and many other psychosomatic diseases are increasingly manifesting among the working people. These problems can aggravate if they are not addressed suitably before it is too late. This is where counselling can be of immense help. Counselling can not only mitigate the kind of problems mentioned above, but also could have pre-empted them if he was counselled properly and at the right time. However, if a problem is found to be beyond the scope of counselling, the person concerned may be advised to seek the services of a psychotherapist or a psychiatrist, as the case may be, without further delay.

The global research suggests that an estimated 1 billion people world-wide live with anxiety and depression, pre-Covid. The pandemic has increased that number by about 27%. According to a WHO report, for every one million Indians, there are just three psychiatrists and even fewer psychologists. Poor work place mental health impacts employee productivity. As mental health is still considered a taboo, it is essential to create a sense of empathy and awareness, as part of promoting an open culture to eliminate the stigma. In this context, counselling of staff members will be a step in the right direction to alleviate the mental health problems.

In the banking context, a superior can act as a counsellor to the employees under his charge who might be facing psychological or emotional problems. But, for this, he must not only have knowledge of the nuances of counselling but also have experience of applying it in daily life. By using his counselling skills to heal employees suffering from various emotional and other problems, he can not only add immense value to his human relations functions but also contribute to organisational development. Learning and practising counselling is not a tough job at all. With a keen interest in people, empathetic understanding, good communication skills and strong will power, even an ordinary person can become a good counsellor and add enormous value to his leadership functions.

It is worth emphasising here that it is very important to possess the aforesaid qualities and skills to be a good counsellor. Without them, a counsellor will mostly likely be a failure. A good counsellor on the other hand, can not only impart the necessary knowledge and confidence to employees to solve their problems on their own but also bring about positive behavioural change in any unruly staff member. But, there is a golden rule that a superior must remember while acting as a counsellor. And that is, he must treat all the information and details that he becomes privy to during his conversations and discussions with the counsellee in the strictest confidence and never disclose them to others. Otherwise, the whole process will lose its sanctity and may prove detrimental to the relationship between the counsellor and the counsellee.

Learning counselling

As mentioned earlier, counselling is not at all a difficult job if one has the necessary aptitude and the willingness to learn. The first step is to familiarize oneself with the counselling techniques by reading a good textbook on the subject and thereafter, upgrade and fine tune the knowledge so gained through practical experience. A counsellor's academic qualifications are not necessarily a sure indication of his competence. Scott Peck, a globally renowned psychotherapist, in his celebrated book, "*The Road Less Travelled*", lays great emphasis on human qualities like love, courage and wisdom for therapists and feels that these qualities cannot be certified by academic degrees. He says, "A minimally trained lay therapist who exercises a great capacity to love will achieve psychotherapeutic results that equal those of the very best psychiatrists."

Is counselling new?

Counselling is not a new phenomenon. The *Bhagawad Gita,* written 5000 years ago, is a classical example of counselling. In Chapter VI (5) Krishna says to Arjuna, *"A man should uplift himself by his own self; he should not degrade his self. For this self is its own friend; this self is its own enemy."* This verse clearly implies that your mind can be both your friend; and your enemy. By thinking positively, we can make our mind our friend and by thinking negatively, we can make our mind our enemy.This is the most important and timeless message of *Gita.* Incidentally, this message is also the essence of modern psychological counselling.

The counsellor must give enormous freedom to his client when the latter is to take a decision for solving a problem. The client should not blindly follow the counsellor nor should the counsellor force him to accept a particular solution. As stated earlier, normally, it is not for the counsellor to suggest a solution to a problem. His job is to identify through extensive and intensive sessions with his client the various motivational factors or causes behind the problem faced by the latter and place them before him for taking a decision. If requested, the counsellor can explain to the client the various available solutions and their relative merits or demerits leaving the final solution to the client. But, strictly speaking, it is not part of a counsellor's job which is to empower the client by equipping him with the necessary information, knowledge, insights and skills to solve a problem by himself.

In this context, it is worth recalling Krishna's remarks to Arjuna at the end of the divine discourse in *Bhagawad Gita,* Chapter XVIII (63). Krishna says: "*Thus has wisdom, most secret of all secrets, been given to thee by ME. After exhaustively reflecting about it, act as thou likest.*" Here, in the divine discourse, Krishna exhorts Arjuna to use his free will to meditate again to realise through awakened intuition and act according to his own wisdom, as He has revealed all the secret truths. This empowering and empathetic approach has gained wide acceptance among modern-day counsellors across the world.

THE ROLE OF FORGIVENESS IN COUNSELLING

Forgiveness is the much needed and most neglected human quality which has the potential to create a win-win solution to interpersonal conflicts. It helps to defuse stress, improve health, strengthen the ruptured relations, avoid costly litigation and even prevent the disastrous consequences of suicides. Counsellors can suggest their clients to choose the option of forgiveness as it is mentally liberating for both the parties involved in the conflict. Forgiveness may appear to be a giving process, but it is a receiving process too. Forgiveness extinguishes vengeance against the other person and bring about lasting peace and tranquillity in the lives of individuals. Clearly, both the receiver and the giver immensely gain from the act of forgiveness. As the timeless saying goes, 'To err is human, to forgive is divine'.

Though counselling is not a panacea for all problems, it can be of much help to bank officials in finding synergistic and workable solutions to their own personal problems as well as those of others. It is indeed a great value addition to their repertoire of skills which can be used anywhere and everywhere to help people fighting their inner demons. ***"Helping one person might not change the world, but it could change the world for one person." -Anonymous***

CHAPTER 10

Customer Service : Make It A Way Of Life

"There is only one boss: the customer. And he can fire everybody in the company from the chairman down, simply by spending his money somewhere else."
- Sam Bolton.

Customers are the very purpose of an organisation. Healthy and prolonged existence of an organisation is validation of the continued patronage of its customers. It is worth recalling here what Gandhi ji said about the importance of customers to a business- "A customer is the most important visitor on our premises. He is not dependent on us. We are dependent on him. He is not an interruption in our work - he is the purpose of it. He is not an outsider to our business. He is a part of it. We are not doing him a favour by serving him. He is doing us a favour by giving us the opportunity to do so."

The above statement of Gandhi ji is as relevant today as it was when it was made. Therefore, any problem coming in the way of offering quality customer service must be resolved at the earliest. Serving the customers diligently is an organisational responsibility, not a choice. Without customers, there is no organisation; without organisation, there is no business and without business, there is no income or profit. And without business, the employees and the stakeholders in the business and their families may find the going tough. Such is the nature of the dependence of a business on its customers.

In the case of banking business, the bankers are not simply maintaining the accounts of the customers. They act as the trustees of the customers' money while also helping the growth of businesses and industries by lending the money held in the depositors' accounts, taking all precautions to ensure that moneys lent come back with interest. Profit earned from such operations are used for further development of a bank's business by opening new branches and by promoting and marketing the bank's products; for payment of shareholder dividends and salaries of the employees and for meeting the dues under bad and doubtful accounts etc.

IMPORTANCE OF CUSTOMER SERVICE

It's ultimately customer service that makes you stand out

Customer service is important in all industries. However, in the case of service industries like banking, the quality of customer service can make or break a business because of the following reasons:

A banking product being a service product is intangible. Because of this reason, to the buyer (customer), it is inseparable from the seller (the clerk or the officer selling the product), his knowledge about the product, his presentation, his friendliness or the lack of it, his behaviour, his helpful nature or the lack of it, his interpersonal skills etc. All these become a part of the product as far as the buyer is concerned. Consequently, the overall success of the product will depend as much on the product features as it does on the qualities of the clerk or officer selling it as perceived by the customer.

One of the strategies used by banks to market their products is called 'product strategy'. Under this, a bank first makes a thorough assessment of what the market needs or what a niche segment of the market needs and based on that, launches a product with the right kind of innovations. Let's suppose, a product so launched becomes highly successful because of the features appealing to the targeted sections of customers. The bank will initially try to sell this product to reap the benefits of the first-mover advantage. But, the first-mover advantage does not last forever. Sooner or later, a lot of other banks too may launch identical products. This means that the first-mover advantage no more works for the bank which has pioneered the product. Now, with a number of banks offering the same product, the quality customer service becomes the differentiating factor, who wins in the market.

Customer expectation

Customer service is an evolving and dynamic concept. It is impacted by a number of variables including the state of the competition, the nature of the market, the profile of the average customer, the business environment and so on. Amidst this, one thing that does not change is the expectation of the quality customer service. And if the bank fails to meet this expectation, the customer will not think twice before he goes elsewhere, even if it means paying a higher price for the same product.

Happy experience

In customer service, the satisfying factors will not remain static for long, Therefore, the staff who man the delivery points must always ensure a happy and wholesome experience to the customers, if necessary, by changing gears. They must smile from their heart and display attentiveness, promptness, and empathetic understanding of the customer's perspective. Most customers hate indefinite delay when they call the customer service helpline. They equally hate having to speak to a robot. What they precisely want is to solve the problem, by talking to someone who has the knowledge and the patience to listen. If this is done properly and empathetically, most customers would be satisfied and treat it as a happy experience.

When the grievance is not addressed promptly, they may take up the matter to the next authority within the bank or outside it. Effective mechanisms have been put in place by the Government of India, the RBI and the individual banks to ensure that the complaints received are resolved promptly. The banks should never look at complainants as enemies. Prompt redressal of customers' grievance is their legitimate right. Complaints received must be viewed as feedbacks and they should be dealt with in the right spirit.

Moment of truth

The customers' perception of service quality is based on their encounters with the Bank. Every time when they contact the Bank, the employees with the help of technologies, create a positive or negative impression. The customers view them as service moments. Moment of truth simply means a time when something is tested or when important decisions are made. In other words, the brief critical incidents such as handling conflict, making decisions, problem solving etc are known as "Moment of Truth". The term "Moment of Truth" is associated with Jan Carlsen, who believes that in competition the individual makes the difference.

"Moment of Truth" is a dynamic force with a potential to fuel self-reinforcing relationships. Every interaction can be transformed into special moments and even a brief interaction can be turned into an opportunity for enhancing bank's service credibility. It should be done skillfully and positively by the clerk in the counter. Precisely, it is the quality interactions which really differentiate their service efficiency and it is in such moments the customer decides to continue or discontinue his relationship with the bank.

CUSTOMER SERVICE CHALLENGES

Keeping one's promise

"Neither over-promise nor under-deliver" should be the motto of anyone dealing with customer service. However, in order to bag a new business or to stave off an unpleasant situation, people do tend to over-promise, but when delivery moment comes, they fail to honour the promise. Such false promises can best be avoided, as loss of credibility will affect the individual who gives the false promise and the organization as a whole. The smart thing to do would be to stick to making reasonable promises only and over-deliver if one can, so that the customer gets not just a pleasant surprise but a moment of "Customer delight".

Explaining a product to the customer

Employees have the bounden duty to sell the bank's products as much as possible. Every bank has a variety of deposit and loan products to offer. The frontline staff should be familiar with all the features and benefits of these products, as customers may have only some vague ideas about them. The staff should first patiently listen to the customer, posing queries wherever needed. After identifying his needs, he can suggest the details of the product which is most suitable for him. If more than one product matches customer's needs, he can distinctly differentiate between the features and benefits of each product.

Keep time line and avoid service delay

A service delayed is as bad as service denied and should never be allowed to happen. Today's customers are highly conscious of their rights and the value of their time. They also appreciate transparency in transactions carried out by the bank. In view of this, banks need to ensure that customers are not only extended prompt and quality service but also kept posted with information on matters like service charges, cheque book charges etc debited to their accounts. Further, banks should ensure that all the officers/clerks manning the delivery points are equipped with up-to-date information on various products and other matters of relevance to the customers.

Avoid Insensitivity

A banker must not forget that customers normally keep their liquid assets, the most important and precious part of their wealth, with banks. This money at the bank is the first line of defense for the customer in crisis situations and gives him a feeling of security, contentment, prosperity and peace. When a crisis strikes, a customer may be compelled to withdraw this money, wholly or partly. On such occasions, the banker should try to go out of his way to help the customer in every possible manner. Rude and insensitive behavior, surly looks and avoiding eye contact with such customers should be eschewed at any cost. It must be clearly remembered that in this age of internet and social media, a dissatisfied customer has the potential to cause immense damage to a bank's image. Through word of mouth as well as WhatsApp and Facebook posts, he can inform a large number of people of his bad experience with the bank. News about negative events tends to move very fast. Therefore, a banker needs to be always mindful of the damaging consequences of any failure on his part to extend satisfactory service to the customer.

Don't be argumentative

Extending quality customer service will never be easy as each customer is unique and his expectations too are different. No matter, how hot-tempered and abusive a customer is, one should make it a point to stay polite throughout and avoid speaking in a loud voice. Being polite or composed not only gets you the respect of the customer but it rubs-off customer's negative attitude.

People rarely think alike. Therefore, occasional difference of opinion with customers is natural. Never try to shout him or her down. Always, give the customer a chance to say what he has in mind without interrupting him. This will not only defuse his tension but also make him more positively inclined towards you. After hearing the customer, if you still think you have a better idea or solution to offer, share it with him as your perspective. And if your solution has already worked with other people, make a mention of this fact to him. In this way you can amicably convert the customer to your viewpoint. And if you think that what the customer says is correct, accept the same without reservations, instead of standing on prestige.

Be empathetic

Empathy is one of the most essential qualities for anyone dealing with customer service. People with empathy have the ability to temporarily step into the shoes of another person, and look at things from the latter's perspective and think like him. This quality enables one to consider an issue from the customer's perspective besides one's own and arrive at an unbiased and objective solution.

Handling angry customers

When faced with an angry and unreasonable customer, some of us are likely to lose our temper and try to pay back the customer in the same coin. Never do that. Anger not only spoils your reputation, it is also likely to have a damaging effect on the reputation of your bank. Anger rarely leads to a lasting solution. It only ends up leaving a trail of stress and bitterness on both sides. The following are some time-tested golden sentences which have been found effective while handling angry customers.

"*You are right*": One of the most effective ways to calm an angry customer is to say these golden words to him in the right way. By doing it, you are validating his feelings and viewpoint and telling him that you are on his side.

a. *'I am sorry"* – These are another set of golden words to pacify an angry customer. But, they should be spoken with all sincerity and in a personalized way. These words do not mean that you are admitting your mistake. It simply conveys that you are feeling bad about it.
b. *"I too would feel frustrated if I were in your position."* - Customers often get angry when a solution is delayed or when no one cares for their plight. In such a situation, the customer needs an assurance that you and your organization are empathetic to him. Words like "I too would feel frustrated if I were in your position." said with due earnestness will go a long way in assuaging the customer's feelings." *(For further reading on managing anger, please refer Chapter 8 'Maintaining good health and Managing stress' of this book.")*.

Leveraging computerized services to minimize complaints

Today, most common banking transactions like drawing cash, making payments after shopping, sending remittances through IMPS/NEFT/RTGS etc. can be done without entering the portals of a bank, by using channels like ATMs, Internet Banking, Mobile Banking and so on. In view of the aforesaid, banks should take necessary customer education initiatives to encourage more and more customers to move from the conventional modes of banking to the various online and digital banking services where human intervention is 'nil' or minimal. This shift will benefit both the customer and the banks. For the customer, it will mean more efficient and hassle-free delivery of services. For the banks, it will mean less number of complaints to handle, reduction in the servicing cost of accounts and more time to spend on marketing and recovery-related tasks.

If one desires lasting loyalty and goodwill of customers, there is no strategy more effective to achieve that than extending excellent service to them. The rationale for that is to be found in human psychology as beautifully summed up in the following lines by Maya Angelou, the gifted American poet, storyteller and civil rights activist: ***"I have learned that people will forget what you said, people will forget what you did, but people will never forget how you made them feel".***

CHAPTER 11

Profit Maximisation : The Right Way

Pahom was a hard-working farmer who lived in the nineteenth century Russia. He had sufficient land with him to grow crops on and lead a happy and satisfied life. Yet, he aspired for more land in order to ensure a better life for himself and his family. One day, he learnt of an offer made by the King. Under this offer, for only 1000 roubles, anyone could gain ownership of as much land as he could walk around on foot in a day subject to the condition that he should be able to make it back to the starting point by sunset the same day. In the event of failure to do so, he would lose the entire amount of 1000 roubles invested.

*Pahom, started walking at the appointed time on the specified day and covered quite a lot of land. Each time he felt tired and thought of stopping and going back to the starting point, the desire to maximise his gains held him back. He covered so much distance but finally, getting back to the starting point before sunset looked really difficult. Though desperate he did not give up. He quickened his pace and started to run. He could now see the finish line. By exerting all his energies, the farmer made his final dash to the finish line only to fall over it, dead. His grieving servant now had to take his spade and start digging Pahom's grave, long enough and wide enough to receive the dead body. Pahom thus found his final resting place. Tolstoy ends the story with the following lines- **"Six feet from his head to his heels was all that he needed."***

(Summarised version of Tolstoy's famous short story titled ***'How much land does a man need?'***)

Sky is the limit-- Really?

Organizational growth and maximization of profit are the buzzwords of the times we live in. Growth stories of individuals and organizations today are built around captivating catch-phrases like 'dream big', 'sky is the limit', 'soaring heights' and so on. Our achievement orientation today knows no bounds, notwithstanding the fact that everything in the universe is limited by Nature's law. Even the public sector undertakings which operated on 'no profit, no loss' basis in the past have now been compelled to join the bandwagon of profit maximisation. Organisations run after the goal of profit mindlessly. Once they reach the goal, they find it is gone; once they fail, they go and go on. No doubt, profit is indispensable. It is the legitimate return on the investment and entrepreneurial efforts of the promoters of a business. That said, it must be noted that like with other things in life, there are always two ways of making profits - the right way and the wrong way. The latter is never good for any individual or business in the long run.

Rampant hunger for profits

Mahatma Gandhi once famously said, "The world has enough for everyone's need, but not enough for everyone's greed." But, there do not seem to be many takers for the Mahatma's cautionary advice today. Whether it is for individuals or businesses, industries or service organizations, putting profit before lives is the order in the business world today. Excessive greed for profits adversely affects not just the customers and the society at large but also becomes counterproductive for that business itself in the long run. The following examples bear this out.

Agriculture was a virgin domain in the old days. Today, farmers in their bid to maximise their yields resort to use of chemical manures and pesticides beyond the permissible level, which are often highly toxic. The toxicity gets passed on to the products too. Regular use of such toxic farm products can lead to cancer, kidney failure and many other health issues. As a result, today, in many countries, more and more consumers are moving away from such products and shifting to those which are grown without the use of chemical manures and pesticides. The fruits, vegetables, grains, milk and meats of today are not what they were a few generations ago. No one can eat enough fruits and vegetables to supply his system with minerals he requires for a perfect health.

In the olden days, doctors believed that their first duty was to educate the masses not to take medicines unnecessarily. But, today the 'maximising-profit-at-any-cost' culture has changed all that. Patients admitted to speciality hospitals for seemingly minor ailments are often subjected to various kinds of diagnostic tests and administered costly medicines even if they are not necessary. There are also cases where patients are made to stay in hospitals even after they have recovered. All these unethical practices have pushed up the cost of medical treatment beyond the reach of the common man. Because of the aforesaid, in many states, the respective state governments have had to intervene and lay down limits on the amounts that hospitals can charge for treatment of various diseases.

The banking sector too finds itself infected by the same culture of 'maximising-profit-at-any-cost'. Traditionally, a bank's income consisted of interest on loans and advances, interest and dividends earned on various government and rated securities, fee-based income from services offered like remittances, forex operations, issue of bank guarantees and letters of credit, provision of safe deposit locker facility, service charges on accounts maintained etc. Ideally, profit must derive from business productivity, not by arbitrarily increasing prices in a favourable market environment.

Of late, many banks have started levying charges for a series of ordinary banking services; charges collected may seem to be little but added up to a huge sum over time. Services offered through ATM are charged substantially. They also earn commission on distribution of third-party products like insurance and mutual funds. No doubt, non-interest income generating activities are very important for banks today. There is nothing wrong in a bank trying to increase its fee-based income by employing various means as long as it is done in an ethical and fair manner. The ordinary customers with abysmal level of financial literacy are unable to comprehend the complicated rules and calculations of the charges. In their relentless pursuit of more and more fee-based income banks have been showing less and less concern for banking ethics as exemplified by the following experience of a bank customer.

Very recently, I visited a private bank branch on an urgent business. While I was sitting inside the Branch Manager's cabin, a Savings Bank customer approached the Branch Manager with a request for allotment of a safe deposit locker to him. Putting on his best behaviour, the Branch Manager apprised the customer of all the related formalities including opening of a fixed deposit account of Rs.25,000 in the name of the customer (hirer) which would be pledged to the bank to cover the risk of non-payment of locker rent and taking an insurance policy for Rs. 5,00,000 on the life of the customer (hirer) from one of the private insurers with whom the bank had a tie-up arrangement. The customer was agreeable to opening the fixed deposit account. But, he was clearly not willing to take the insurance policy as his life was already sufficiently insured with LIC. The customer pleaded with the Branch Manager to waive the relevant requirement but to no avail. The BM expressed helplessness as he was not authorised to waive the requirement. Finally, after a few more futile attempts to convince the BM, the customer walked out of the cabin in a huff, disappointment and displeasure writ large on his face.

Having observed all this, deep within, I was feeling upset by the apparently unfair insistence on the insurance policy by the BM. As if sensing what was going in my mind, the latter turned to me and said, 'I can understand his problem but I am helpless. I can't change the bank's policy'. Obviously, he was referring to the policy of the bank which mandated a new insurance policy on the life of the customer from the private insurer as a pre-condition for allotment of the locker. The motive behind such practices is questionable. Clearly, the bank's policy had no place for banking ethics.

How excessive profit-seeking becomes counterproductive

1. Chances of overreach

A business solely driven by the objective of profit maximisation will have a tendency to overreach itself and landing in trouble as a consequence. For example, a businessman may decide to scale up his business substantially at one go for the sake of increasing his profits without trying to make a realistic assessment of the expected demand. In the process, he may spend a lot on increasing his inventories and hiring additional staff. If the expected demand does not materialise, instead of making more profits, the business may see its profits plunge because of the unsold inventories and bloated payroll.

2. *Adverse effect on long-term sustainable goals*

Too much of profit-seeking often results in shifting of focus from long-term sustainable goals to short-term profits which may cost the business dearly. For example, a person running a restaurant may try to increase his profits by switching to lower-quality ingredients. In the short term, his profits may go up. But, the switch to lower-quality ingredients will be reflected in the quality of the final products too, which will upset the customers who normally buy them. Gradually, the restaurant will start losing business to competitors. Adopting such shortcuts for making more profits will eventually lead to existential crisis of businesses.

The key ethical points for any business, small or big, to be internalised and put into practise are: decent work and responsibility to ensure quality service, backed by principled and value orientated action, will invariably result in enhanced profitability, sustainable growth and overall well-being of the stakeholders.

3. *Does not consider the time value of money*

The profit maximization principle simply states that the higher the profit, the better the performance of a business. If the profit is related to a time frame, the principle ignores the fact that the value of a certain unit of money does not remain constant due to factors like inflation etc. For example, the value of Rs.100 today not going to have the same value if it is received five years later.

4. *Exploitation of labour*

A firm driven by the aim of profit maximisation tends to end up exploiting its workers in order to cut down on the cost of production. Demands for higher pay are just brushed aside; strikes are suppressed. Such tactics will dip the motivation level of the workers to a point where they just do what is sufficient to avoid punishment. As a result, work quality and productivity will suffer; the firm's profitability is likely to hit a plateau.

5. *Economic and social inequalities*

Unfettered pursuit of profits by businessmen tends to lead to more and more economic and social inequalities in society. While a miniscule section of the society gains control of most of the resources of the country, the majority may have to endlessly struggle to make ends meet. Egalitarian values take a backseat. This kind of situation can lead to high crime rates and social unrest. The aforesaid excessive profit-seeking designs and its consequences are universal in every conceivable area of business operations today.

What should Indian banks do to increase their profitability?

1. Frauds and Bad loans eating into profits - Finding the right solutions: Many people know about how banks make profit but only a few know how the profits are utilised. Generally, a portion of the profit is ploughed back and utilised for the development of the organization. The rest of it is mainly used for paying dividends to the shareholders, creating reserves for the bad and doubtful debts and for writing off bad debts. The staggering statistics put out by the Reserve Bank of India reveals that between April 1, 2015 and December 31, 2021, banks across the country were defrauded to the tune of Rs. 2.5 lakh crore. Further, on 13th December 2022, the Finance Minister, Nirmala Sitharaman reported to have informed the Parliament that banks have written off bad loans worth Rs.10,09,511 crore in the last five financial years. *(Source: Times of India dated 29.3.2022 and 14.12.2022).*

The curious paradox is that most of these staggering sums on account of bad debts and frauds are eventually written-off from the hard-earned profits of the banks. Given the aforesaid harsh reality, it is doubtful if steps like reducing the number of PSBs through mergers etc. will make any difference to the problems of NPAs and frauds faced by the banking sector. The banks should detect signs of sickness early so that necessary recovery steps could be initiated in a timely manner. The legal remedies available under relevant Acts of the central and state governments ie. Securitization and Reconstruction of Financial Assets and Enforcement of Security Interest Act (SARFAESI) 2002, the Debt Recovery Tribunals Act (DRT), 1993, Insolvency and Bankruptcy Code, 2016, Revenue Recovery Act as appropriate should be fully utilised for effecting recoveries. The governments and the courts on their part need to take urgent steps to minimise pendency of cases involving moneys lent by banks.

Frauds lead to reputational, operational and business risk for banks and undermine customers' trust in the banking system. Strictly enforcing internal guidelines, including compliance measures and those issued by Reserve Bank of India and other bodies/departments concerned from time to time, is likely to go a long way in bringing down the incidence of such crimes by anti-social elements.

2. Behaviour - a key determinant of success

Modern research studies show that high productivity and profits are closely linked to the behavioural patterns in organizations. In a recent study on 'social mindedness', conducted across 31 countries by Niels Van Doesum, a Dutch academic, the Japanese came on top in the matter of showing small acts of kindness. But, India came third from the bottom. The study reveals that little things like kindness and niceness improve productivity and profitability. It is a well-known truth that behavioural sophistication of the workforce is extremely important in service industry like banks. Another finding from the study is that in a high-trust society, there is little need for suppressive laws and similarly, a high-trust work atmosphere in an organisation reduces the need for rigorous controls.

In today's highly competitive environment, the branch managers and officers often have to put in extra hours of work for canvassing business, augmenting non-interest income etc., many times ignoring their private and social commitments. In the case of women officers, the work-life imbalance is more pronounced in view of the crucial role they play in the upbringing of children. The aforesaid facts warrant an enlightened and empathetic approach from the side of the management. Sadly, the traditional high-handed and arrogant approach is still followed by the majority of managers. Some believe that instilling fear in the subordinates is the key to get results from them. Instilling fear not only spoils inter-personal relations between the management and the subordinates but also leads to trust deficit between the two sides. Such a situation not only takes a toll on the health of the people concerned on both sides, but also impact productivity and profit-earning capacity of the organization. No wonder, it will hasten large scale attrition across different staff categories.

It is high time Indian banks started practising seriously the timeless behavioural principles like integrity, compassion, empathy and commitment in their dealings with the staff, customers, the general public and other stake holders, as given in Chapter 1. This is not to say that these principles are alien to Indian banks. In this context, one is reminded of the well-known proverb: *'For want of a nail, the Kingdom was lost'.* The proverb is based on a story about a battle during which the loss of a nail in a horseshoe leads to the death of a horse, which leads to the death of the rider, which leads to the loss of the battle, which in turn leads to the King concerned losing his whole kingdom. Like the nail, the principles mentioned above may appear unimportant to many people. But, when one takes a long-term and holistic view of the matter, it will be clear that they have a major impact on the growth and success of an organization.

3. Branch as a profit-centre

This concept has been successfully used by many banks in India and abroad to improve their profits. The lion's share of the profit of a bank is earned by branches. Ideally, every branch should be acting as a profit-centre which means it will have to independently plan for its projected profits by figuring out how much deposits to raise and in what proportion.

The funds management function should get transferred from the higher offices to branches in order to ensure optimum profitability from operations, by appropriate mechanism. For example, some branches may have high deposit potential but low loan potential to absorb the funds available to them through deposits. While there may be others who may have high loan potential but low deposit potential. In such a scenario, there needs transfer of funds from the first category of branches (high deposit potential) to the second category (high loan potential), through Transfer Pricing Mechanism. This is a method in place to reward the first category of branches for mobilising funds at their cost which are subsequently profitably deployed in other branches, thus benefiting the bank as a whole.

4. Customer service

A banking product being intangible in nature, the success or failure of a product depends a lot on the kind of service extended to a customer at the branch level. Therefore, a bank should ensure that there is no compromise on customer service. (Please read *Customer service, Chapter-10).*

5. Cost consciousness and avoidance of wasteful expenditure

A bank should frame necessary policies and guidelines to spread a culture of cost consciousness across the organization. The top executives of a bank should lead by example when it comes to cutting costs and avoiding wasteful expenditure.

6. Regular audits and inspections

A bank should put in place a system of regular inspections and audits of branches in order to ensure that any act of malfeasance or misconduct is detected at the earliest so that damage to the bank's interest is minimised.

7. Focus on increasing market share

Banks should create a list of their clients and seek their help to extend their (banks') reach to more and more potential customers. Another way of doing this is through community organizations.

8. Reduce employee turnover and improve employee satisfaction

A satisfied employee is always likely to contribute more to the development of a bank than a dissatisfied one. In view of this, banks should ensure that employees are offered enough growth opportunities and material benefits eg. competitive salaries, flexible work schedules, five-day week, ESOP, higher education reimbursement programmes etc.

9. Make your products more and more reliable

For any product to succeed, it must stay reliable at all times. The products must be constantly updated/refined in the light of feedback received from users. Banks should collect and process customer feedback and ensure that the departments concerned initiate suitable action without delay.

10. Corporate ethics and more active engagement in Corporate Social Responsibility (CSR) activities

The ethics practised by a company has a big role to play in shaping the public perception about it. A well-managed CSR programme can do wonders to the brand value of a company. A case in point is the Tata Group. People appreciate the Tata group of companies not only for the high quality of their products but also for the laudable CSR activities they have been engaging in for the greater good of the society at large.

The enhanced brand value and the positive public image accruing to a company due to its CSR activities ultimately has a positive impact on the sales of its products as well. Recent studies indicate that CSR activities also affect employees' attachment and pride in their organization and thus, affect their work-related attitudes and behaviour too. In view of the above, banks should try to engage actively in CSR activities. The following lines by Henrietta Newton Martin succinctly convey how important corporate ethics and CSR activities are to a company.

"A business that thinks beyond 'profit making' and 'profit maximisation' by incorporating corporate ethics and contributes to the society at large, through its well-defined corporate social responsibility policy, is the one that will withstand the test of time and meet sustainable growth in the market. I believe its curve will never grow flat for a good number of years and may meet only merger or acquisitions but rarely a winding up."

....

CHAPTER 12

Branch Manager : The Woes, Opportunities And Challenges

"A leader is one who knows the way, goes the way, and shows the way." -John Maxwell

Traditionally, a bank manager enjoys very high respect in society. To an average customer, he is the personification of the bank he works for and the kingpin of the branch he heads, who directly controls every activity in the branch. For all practical purposes, the hierarchical structure of the bank management has no relevance to the average customer. Given the aforesaid, the branch manager has to constantly strive to meet the standards the customer has set for him. The bank too sets very high standards for him and has ever-rising expectations of him. He is expected to possess excellent leadership qualities to command the respect of his team. He must be a good motivator with the ability to influence the team members positively. He is expected to be knowledgeable, to be influential, to be good at marketing and so the list goes on. But, our focus here is on the leadership role of the branch manager.

The leadership role of a branch manager extends to almost all functions performed by him. Trueleadership can be transformational. A true leader is always a keen observer of the performance of his team members. He believes in giving direct feedback to them individually without fear or favour. He tries to boost the morale, self-confidence and positive energy of team members. Where he notices any kind of deficiency in performance, he counsels the team member concerned in a constructive way so that course correction is achieved without any way demoralizing him/her. A leader must care for the people around him passionately and encourage them to grow. He must be proactive, trustworthy, humble, compassionate and smart enough to earn the respect of the team members. In view of the importance of the leadership role for a branch manager, in this chapter, he has also been referred to as manager-leader at some places to emphasize the point.

Qualities of a good manager-leader

Designating a person as a branch manager cannot automatically make him a good branch manager. For that, he or she must possess certain abilities. If the person lacks them, he must work hard to acquire them. Some of the essential the essential qualities are briefly discussed below:

1. Ability to deal with people

A manager is expected to get things done by staff at the branch. Besides knowing everything about the work they do, he must also have the knowledge of the human psychology which will enable him to grasp their sentiments, aspirations, strengths and weaknesses.

2. Ability to inspire

Though it may sound a little strange, a successful manager is one who does minimum work himself and gets maximum work done by his staff. That manager is a failure who attempts to do everything himself. His job should be to develop and inspire every team member in such a way that he (team member) not only discharges his functions efficiently but also strives to upgrade his skills constantly. Needless to say, to inspire his staff, a branch manager requires effective communication and man-management skills.

3. Intelligence

A branch manager must have the ability to understand the main problem quickly. He may not be a master of everything, but he must have adequate knowledge of all the important areas of banking including their financial, technical and legal aspects. If there are senior personnel well-versed with the nitty-gritty of the issue to be decided, they should be consulted wherever necessary, before taking a decision. But, the final decision should always rest with the branch manager.

4. Sense of responsibility

Authority and responsibility normally go together. A manager must be conscious of his authority as well as responsibility. Since he has got authority over the subordinates, he is responsible for their performance too. Shirking of responsibility is not expected of a branch manager.

5. *Ability to take right decisions*

A manager-leader must have the power of judgment, self-confidence, imagination and creative abilities. He should be able to take the right decision quickly after assessing the merits or otherwise of the different options available. And, once he takes a decision, he should have the confidence to stick to it and make a success of it.

6. *Ability to motivate*

A manager-leader should be able to inspire the team members to give their best to their job and thus contribute to the organizational goals. In the process, the team members also get the opportunity to realise their potential to the maximum. It is the responsibility of the branch manager to turn his team into a highly motivated and close-knit group of people where everyone identifies with the team and its goals and takes pride in belonging to it.

Besides the above, the branch managers as leaders, are advised to understand and internalize the qualities of a leader discussed in detail in Chapter 1.

Certain practical do's and don'ts

A manager-leader should remember to follow the rules mentioned below *vis-a-vis* his subordinates.

a. Assignment of duties and responsibilities to each employee should be definite and clear-cut.
b. No change should be made in the scope or responsibilities of a position without a definite understanding to that effect on the part of all concerned.
c. No employee occupying a single position should be subject to orders from more than one source.
d. Criticism of subordinates should be done privately. In no case, a subordinate should be criticised in the presence of another employee.

What more is expected of a manager-leader in the present-day context?

Creativity and out-of-the-box thinking

He needs to act as a thought-leader for the team and encourage creativity and out-of-the-box thinking. An eternal truth is that change is inherent in nature and it is the only thing constant in life. Banking too need not always tread the beaten track. A branch manager should not just remain satisfied with staff members *doing things right*. He must also try to ignite their latent creativity and innovativeness so that they are also able to find the *right things to do* and do them. The talent and innovative skills of employees can be utilized by branch managers to find solutions to various problems faced by the branch or to find ways to do things faster and better or to improve the recovery of NPAs and so on. They can, for this purpose, form 'Think tanks' or 'strategic groups' in their respective branches. Such groups should be tasked with holding brainstorming sessions from time to time on issues identified by the branch manager and give their suggestions. These suggestions should be forwarded by branches to the ROs periodically. The ROs in turn should screen the individual suggestions and send the selected ones to Head Office for consideration. The Head Office in turn should examine the suggestions received at their level and select those which can be taken up for implementation. To encourage greater participation under the scheme, the H.O. should have in place a system of rewarding the top three suggestions. Besides tapping latent talent and skills of its employees, this process also helps banks to identify the future leaders in the making.

Avoiding position consciousness

As leaders, bank managers and officers should not be over-conscious of their grade or scale or position. Serving the customers is the common denominator of most of the functions carried out by the different functionaries in a branch. In that sense, the branch manager stands on the same pedestal as his subordinates. Given this, the branch manager should not remain aloof from the action taking place outside his cabin. He must walk through his group, listen to their problems, solve them on real-time basis and generally inspire them to seek excellence in whatever they do. To put it briefly, a branch manager should avoid becoming a 'cabin manager', a derisive expression used by bank employees in India to describe a branch manager who is aloof, withdrawn and confines himself to his cabin most of the time. The branch manager must clearly understand the truth that different designations and grades for various functionaries exist for administrative reasons only and they should never be allowed to lead to divisive class consciousness or ego clashes among the team members in a branch.

IDENTIFYING POTENTIAL BRANCH MANAGERS

It is a fact of life that each individual is unique. Each has his/her own areas of strength as well as weakness too. For example, 'A' may perform excellently as a second line officer but he may turn out to be a failure as branch manager. With 'B", the situation could be the reverse; he may be good as a branch manager but mediocre as a second line officer. This aspect needs to be kept in mind while posting officers as branch managers.

Posting officers lacking the required aptitude and abilities as branch managers will be counterproductive to the bank concerned. Therefore, such postings must be made only after properly evaluating their suitability for the job, taking into account the various functional parameters. As the regional heads are the best judges in the matter, the Regional Offices should maintain a list of potential branch managers in each region on an ongoing basis under functional parameters like integrity, leadership qualities, dynamism, knowledge level, communication skills, empathetic response, inter-personal relationship skills, resilience, punctuality, discipline etc. Each RO should send a copy of their list to the Personnel Department at H.O. who in turn can use it for taking decisions with regard to placement and training of the officers included in the list.

ENABLING BRANCH MANAGERS TO PERFORM BETTER

Functional challenges

Fundamentally, the banks function as intermediaries; they do their business with the deposits raised from the public. Over the years, the basic functions of a commercial bank viz. accepting deposits and lending money, have witnessed multi-dimensional changes. As a result, a branch manager today has to oversee a mind-boggling array of functions covering the areas of deposits, advances, business development, ATM payments, customer service, complaints of customers, functioning of computers, branch administration, NPA management and recoveries etc. Under the current dispensation separate verticals are functioning in many banks to sanction loans. They take care of appraisal, the sanctioning, documentation etc and are working in silos. The branch manager and his teams are increasingly focusing their efforts on marketing.

On top of all this, the branch manager has to work under the constant pressure of targets and deadlines set by the controlling offices. The branch manager is not only responsible for his own acts of omission and commission, but he also has constructive responsibility for the acts of omission and commission of his subordinates. Insider accounts from many banks indicate that a large number of incumbent branch managers are not happy doing their job because of the multiple challenges they have to deal with on a daily basis and the consequent near-complete absence of work-life balance in their lives. Not surprisingly, many of them either opt for premature retirement or die in harness as a consequence of various ailments contracted during the long years of their banking career, with tension and strain as constant companions. Still more worrying are the increasing number of cases where branch managers/officers, unable to cope with the relentless challenges of their job, surrender to despair and even commit suicide. The prevailing unhappy situation is often exacerbated by the following facts.

In the past, normally, only officers with the necessary aptitude and fairly long years of proven experience were posted as branch heads. However, at present, due to mass retirements of senior officers, officers with limited experience and exposure too are being given the charge of branches, in both PSBs as well as private sector banks. The situation is such that even a just-promoted officer in scale II, may get posted as branch manager of a frontline city branch. An important thing to note in this context is that to do justice to the post of a branch manager, one needs not just physical maturity but also mental and emotional maturity which comes only through practical experience of working in different areas of banking and dealing with different kinds of customers and staff for a number of years. Such experience helps sharpen one's intellect and improve interpersonal skills and confidence, which are essential qualities for the role of a branch manager. If an officer not sufficiently equipped for the role of branch manager is thrust into it, it could dent his morale forever and also adversely impact the effectiveness of his team. The consequences of such a scenario are:

a. Customer service is adversely affected.
b. Productivity and profitability of the staff are drastically reduced.
c. Work-life balance of branch manager and his team members is disrupted.
d. Branch manager's morale is badly spoiled.

Given the above, the following steps are urgently called for.

Rationalising the workload

It is high time banks thought of reducing the heavy workload that the present system imposes on the branch manager. Let's discuss a possible solution to the problem, in the following lines, which has already been tried out by some banks in a limited way and for a different reason.

Specialization is the order of the day and for good reason. In the olden days, the family doctor with an MBBS degree was considered good enough to treat any disease contracted by a human being. But, over time, different specialized areas of treatment have evolved for different afflictions that can affect the human body. As a result, today we have specialist doctors with expert knowledge to treat and cure most diseases known to man.

The concept of specialization, as above, is equally relevant to the field of banking. For example, if a branch manager or an officer has to perform varying functions, which are different from each other in the course of a day, where credit-related or recovery-related matters form only a small percentage of the whole, chances of his gaining expertise in these areas will not be high as expertise comes only when one is frequently exposed to a large variety of experiences. In the light of the above, wherever a bank has more than 10 branches, it should consider transferring specialized functions like industrial advances, agricultural advances, retail loans, foreign exchange business etc. to one or more specialized branches dedicated to the specialized areas of banking. Such branches should be barred from handling non-specialized areas of banking. However, at centres having less than 10 branches, the existing arrangement may be allowed to continue.

As mentioned above, some banks have already made a beginning in this regard by designating some branches for exclusively processing, sanctioning and maintaining all retail loan accounts or MSME loan accounts in a specified geographical unit. Similarly, a few banks have also designated some branches as Asset recovery branches exclusively dealing with the follow-up and recovery measures under NPA accounts in a specified geographical unit after taking over such accounts from the sanctioning branches. Though the work handled by these specialized branches may differ, the underlying idea is common to all of them, which is reaping the benefits of specialization. However, it should be noted that this change also serves to reduce the workload of the personnel at non-specialized branches as all the work relating to the specialized areas of banking handled by them earlier would get transferred to specialized branches. This may necessitate some tweaking in the placement policies of banks which are based on the concept of a "well-rounded" banker, well-versed in all areas of banking akin to the concept of "all-rounder" in cricket. This concept may have been relevant in the old days when banking activities were not so complex or specialized. But, it is no more so today when banking covers everything from rural banking to investment counselling to forex dealing to leasing to derivatives to merchant banking and so on. With more and more players trying to enter the areas of specialized banking verticals, banks should try to embrace the 'specialization' mantra wholeheartedly and work towards a wider roll-out of specialized branches in order to remain competitive. The increase in the number of specialized branches will also provide much-needed relief to the community of branch managers who today are groaning under the weight of an excessive workload.

Training and hand-holding new branch managers

Banks need to ensure that officers, newly posted as branch managers, are adequately equipped to discharge their new responsibilities. This can be done through interventions like training programmes, regular handholding and support from ROs and experienced branch managers heading other branches at the centre concerned.

As I prepare to conclude this chapter, a precious bit of advice attributed to Dolly Parton comes to mind: ***"Never get so busy making a living that you forget to make a life".*** One hopes that sooner, rather than later, IBA and the bank managements in India will take necessary and suitable steps to make it possible for bank managers to have a better work-life balance in their lives.

CHAPTER 13

Work-Life Balance : Crafting A Balanced Symphony

"Clients do not come first. Employees come first; If you take care of your employees, they will take care of the client."
- Richard Branson

"Work is a rubber ball. If you drop it, it will bounce back. The other four balls - family, health, friend, integrity - are made of glass. If you drop one of these, it will be irrevocably scuffed, nicked and even shattered."
- Gary Keller

Service to customers is the defining characteristic of any service-oriented industry, including banking. Needless to emphasize, if there is no work-life balance in the lives of the workforce in such industries, quality of the service rendered to customers is going to be the first casualty with disastrous consequences for the business as a whole. In this chapter let us examine some of the ways in which bankers could achieve the right work-life balance and lead happy and purposeful lives while also contributing to the progress of their respective organisations. But, let it be said in the beginning itself that the search for the ideal work-life balance can be fruitful only if there is sufficient appreciation of its importance as well as willingness to work for it on the side of both the employees and the employers.

Importance of work in life

It is through work that we grow and fulfil life's deep-seated emotional needs. Just like a plant needs a fertile piece of land to grow, a bank employee needs the right people and the right ambience around to grow and fulfil his emotional needs. That said, pursuit of work should not mean exclusion of many other equally important things like loyalty to family, relatives, friends and the society at large, concern for the deprived and the underprivileged, doing one's duties as a citizen etc. The trick lies in prioritising life and work in such a way that neither is neglected. Nevertheless, the fact remains that bankers usually invest most of their time and energy on their official work right till they retire from service. In the process, many of them often neglect their roles as husband/wife and/or as father/mother, as the case may be. As a result, in later years, many of them end up leading far-from-happy personal lives. Some also have to suffer the mortification of bringing up children gone astray who have to struggle to get even pass marks in the annual examination at school or college.

HOW TO ACHIEVE WORK-LIFE BALANCE?

A. WHAT CAN AN EMPLOYEE DO?

As mentioned earlier, achieving work-life balance in the life of an employee takes efforts from the sides of both the employee and the employer. Let us first try to examine what all an employee needs to do to achieve work-life balance.

1. Treat work as worship

The first step in the journey to find work-life balance is to have the right attitude to work. Mahatma Gandhi summed up in three simple words- "Work is worship". The great Hindu scripture, *"The Bhagvad Gita"* attach a lot of importance to *'Karma'* (action) in one's life. When Arjuna expressed unwillingness to fight the war of Kurukshetra for various reasons Lord Krishna, the Supreme One, advised as under:

"Karmanye vadhikaraste ma phaleshu kadachana ma karma phalaheturbhuh, matey sangotsva karmani." (The Bhagvad Gita, Chapter 2:47)

("You have a right to *"Karma"* (actions) but never to any fruits thereof. You should never be motivated by the results of your actions nor should there be any attachment to not doing the prescribed activities.")

When you work with passion, involving fully, you can experience joy, success and contentment. Think about a mother working hard in the kitchen for feeding her children and other family members. When she works with the frame of mind of 'what I can give?' instead of 'what I can get?' the result will be sublimely satisfying. When people work wholeheartedly, without expectations, there will be improvement in the profitability and productivity of the organization.

Similarly, when you try to win others, you are creating a distressed loser. But in success you just succeed, you are not creating a loser. It is the mindset that matters. You can bring remarkable change in life when you replicate this idea in every domain of your life.

2. Be proactive and not reactive

The bank staff should be proactive and work smart so as to be able to finish their tasks promptly within the allotted time. A proactive person will not find fault with others or frequently blame the circumstances when things go wrong. He owns responsibility and takes initiative. He makes things happen rather than waiting for things to happen. On the other hand, a reactive person never takes any initiative and merely responds to events and people. Work should always be properly planned and organised around priorities. The department heads, after completing the computer-generated day-end work, can attend to the remaining routine and any work in arrears. The branch head should monitor the progress of outstanding work from time to time. If pendency is due to overload of work, the branch manager should address the issue promptly and ensure equitable distribution of work. Such practices will ensure that no one is overworked at any point of time.

3. Avoid habitual late-sitting after office hours

As against the business and working hours displayed in the branch premises, the actual time spent by an employee every day at work very often turns out to be longer. This happens often due to extra load of work. More hours spent on work need not necessarily be treated as a sign of hard work. Even if you work normal hours or an hour or two more, work mindfully, and be focused, the result will be wonderful. In some cases, the Parkinson's Law will also be in operation, according to which, "Work expands so as to fill the time which is available for its completion." In other words, the time required to do a task often expands to fill the time available to do it. As a result, a worker becomes inefficient and himself becomes the greatest impediment to work-life balance in his life.

Such avoidable late-sitting also takes a toll on the worker's health besides pushing up electricity bills of the organization on account of extra hours of use of lights, fans, and air-conditioners etc. Therefore, an employee should make it a point to avoid unnecessary late-sitting at office.

4. Importance of rest and relaxation

Usually, the human body is at its energetic best in the morning and therefore, this part of the day is best suited for doing all the heavy works. As the day progresses, the energy level starts diminishing. The dip starts taking effect in the afternoon and becomes more pronounced towards the end of the day. To the extent possible, an employee should plan his output according to the diminishing pattern of his energy levels. In other words, one should try to clear the heavy jobs first and then move on to less difficult or less challenging ones as the day progresses. After strenuous working during the day, the body and mind of an employee cry out for rest and relaxation and this cry should be duly heeded. Otherwise, one may have to pay a heavy price in the long run. Therefore, even the most duty-conscious and hard-working employee must understand when to call it a day, after a hard day's work at office. Long hours at work must be balanced by sufficient rest and relaxation at home. The employees should do their best to stay healthy and lead quality lives for their own good as well as the good of their organisation.

5. Don't just work hard, work smart too

Most of the banking-related jobs are mechanical and repetitive in nature and therefore, there is scope for committing mistakes inadvertently. The new generation officers must reimagine the conventional working style and improve their creativity in every conceivable area of their activities. As it has been well said, the mind is like a parachute and it works well when it is opened. The following example may not be out of place here. Counter staff in banks are often approached by customers to fill up pay-in-slips or RTGC/NEFT application forms on their behalf. The staff has to oblige them even if they are in the midst of some more urgent work. Naturally, in such distractive moments, some inadvertent mistakes and errors may happen occasionally. With some timely use of creativity and 'out-of-the-box' thinking such situations can be avoided. For instance, in the aforesaid example, the counter staff can fill up the relevant form once and then ask the customer to take a screenshot of the filled-up form on his/her mobile phone for future reference so that he/she can independently do the filling up the next time. Such simple innovativeness and creativity should become a way of life in order to keep one's working style attuned to the dynamics of work situations in the current era.

6. Remember multi-tasking is a mixed blessing

In simple terms, multitasking is the ability to do more than one task at the same time. Modern research suggests that multitasking often turns out to be disadvantageous and even dangerous. The reason is not far to seek. Our brains normally lack the ability to perform multiple tasks at the same time. What we take as multi-tasking is nothing more than quickly and repeatedly jumping to and fro between jobs leading to more physical exhaustion with no extra benefit to show. Doing a job correctly and properly needs focus and attention. The so-called multi-tasking is most ill-suited when one is aiming at accurate and error-free outcomes. Of course, this is not to say that multi-tasking should not be attempted at all. Definitely, in the case of routine jobs without any financial or other serious implications, multi-task could be an option. But, the bottom line is that one must have complete knowledge of the work one handles before attempting multi-tasking. *(See Chapter 6, 'Knowledge Management').*

7. Delegate where necessary

A lot of work-life balance related problems have their roots in the reluctance of superiors to delegate work even where such delegation is permitted by rules. Sometimes, this happens because the superior does not have sufficient confidence in the delegatee's abilities. Mostly, the reason is the reluctance of the superior to share his/her specialised knowledge with others for fear of losing his/her importance in the scheme of things at the branch/office. Irrespective of the underlying reason, such reluctance to delegate work is not good for either the organization or the superior. The organization suffers when the superior chooses to spend his valuable time and efforts on doing a task which could as well be done by someone lower down in the hierarchy. And for the superior personally, such possessive attachment to any work can only mean work overload leading to work-life imbalance. Any superior, be he a branch manager or a second-line officer, must remember that his job is not to do the work of his subordinates but to ensure that the latter do their jobs efficiently and sincerely and to direct and guide them suitably in this regard. If they lack the requisite attitude or skills for doing a delegated job, the superior should ensure that necessary training etc. is arranged at the earliest to address the issue.

B. WHAT CAN AN ORGANIZATION DO?

1. Ensuring employee's fitness for the job

The attitude, aptitude, knowledge and skills available with an employee to perform his job will always have an important bearing on the overall productivity of the organisation as well as the work-life balance in the employee's life. Someone who does not have adequate competency, but also likely to always harbour an inferiority complex make himself miserable by comparing himself with others. In such cases, the organization needs to identify the specific areas where the employee is weak and address them suitably through counselling, training or other initiatives.

2. Compensation should be linked to risks and challenges

In any organization, there are some jobs which are riskier and more challenging than others. Fairness demands that such jobs carry a proportionately higher compensation vis-a-vis those which do not carry the same kind of risks and challenges. If such differential treatment is not extended, it could demotivate the employees doing the riskier and more challenging jobs, and adversely affect their work-life balance.

3. Role conflict and ambiguity

Role conflict arises when an employee is handling a task in which more than one department is involved, each with its own expectations. Therefore, the employee ends up in a confusing situation, not knowing what is to be prioritised. Role ambiguity arises when an employee is allotted a job which is largely uncharted territory or not clearly defined. This role ambiguity can often cause confusion to the employee as there is no precedent to go by. Banks should ensure that such ambiguity about roles and responsibilities is avoided as it can upset the work-life balance so important in an employee's life, which in turn also impacts the productivity and profitability of the organization.

4. Minimising factors causing stress

Stress can be caused to an executive or an employee by a number of factors. An executive may be under pressure to deliver financial results of the kind expected by the top management. A supervisor may be under pressure to deliver in terms of quality and customer service. Another source of stress could be change of any type which requires an employee to undergo any major kind of adaptation in his life such as temporary lay-off, transfer, change of duties at branch. There can be stress due to long-term factors too, for example, denial of promotion to an employee for an unreasonably long period. An organization needs to ensure that factors leading to over stress for the workforce do not arise and if they are unavoidable, they should be kept at the minimum.

5. Optimum utilisation of computerised services

The cash transaction time or "business hours" in banking parlance during the pre-computerised days was 10 a.m. to 2 PM. Later, after computerisation, it was extended till 4 PM. The aforesaid revised timings still continue in most banks. This in spite of the fact that today, most common banking transactions like drawing cash, making payments after shopping, sending remittances through IMPS/NEFT/RTGS etc. can be done without entering the portals of a bank, by using channels like ATMs, Internet Banking, Mobile Banking etc. In view of the aforesaid, the need of the hour is to revert to the previous business hours of 10 a.m. to 2.00 p.m. with relaxations permitted only for genuinely unavoidable cases. This should be accompanied by necessary customer education initiatives to increase the usage of various online and digital delivery channels mentioned above so as to minimise footfalls inside a branch. This will not only reduce the servicing cost of accounts, but also give the employees more time to attend to back-up work, marketing and work in arrears.

6. Availability of growth opportunities

A job is not just about earning a living by doing something. It also provides an opportunity to individuals to pursue the goal of self-actualisation or realisation of their latent talents and potentialities. For this, every organization should have in place a fair and reliable system for rewarding deserving candidates through promotions. Having in place such a system is one of the most important ways to ensure a proper work-life balance in the lives of the employees and to keep them motivated.

7. Participative style of management

For employees to have better work-life balance, it is necessary that they develop a sense of belonging to the organization. One of the most effective ways to do this is by adopting a participative style of management where the employees are encouraged to make suggestions with regard to work processes, business strategy, marketing etc. and also otherwise contribute to the progress of the branch. Such practices will make the employee feel a part of the whole and strengthen their bonding with the organization; eventually this will enhance the leadership qualities of the staff.

8. Flexible working hours and flexible work settings

Given a choice, most employees would prefer to choose their working hours as well as the location for work i.e. on-site or remote. Such flexibility allows the employees to have better balance between their professional and private lives which in turn help them become more productive. This is more so in the case of women employees. Many organizations have already taken major steps in this direction especially during and after the pandemic phase. Usually, women are forced to work double shift, in home and office. If flexible options like 'work from home' facilities are offered, wherever possible, women's labour force participation can be enhanced.

9. A Case for 5-day week

Three decades ago, during the formative period of full computerization, it was believed that the new endeavour will herald a new age, reducing the manual jobs and the late hour burnouts remarkably. But in contrast, there was exponential growth in business all round. In the backdrop of prolonged Covid-19 swept world over in 2020, 2021 and 2022, the bank employees in India have been seeking introduction of five-day week repeatedly. Currently, what Indian banks effectively follow is 5.5-day week.

Meanwhile, the research findings of Autonomy, a British organisation in its report has stated that the productivity of 2900 staff of the 61 British firms trialling a four-day working week, had maintained that the work-life balance has improved, as a result of the four-day week policy. Some of the employees stated that the extra day off was more important than any pay rise. Taking cue from the foregoing British survey, introduction of full-fledged 5-day week will definitely put more life into the lives of our bankers and hugely enhance the productivity in the Indian banks. Better late than never.

10. Avenues for fun and relaxation

"All work and no play make Jack a dull boy" is an age-old proverb we have all grown up with. The proverb remains as relevant today as when it was first uttered. In fact, today it applies not just to kids but to office-going adults as well. Some fun time during or after working hours helps employees to unwind and feel relaxed at their workplace thus promoting a better work-life balance. The relaxation and fun time must be viewed as a time for unwinding, which eventually help improve their performance and productivity. In the words of Bertrand Russell, "The time you enjoy wasting is not wasted time." No wonder, today some organizations have facilities like coffee dispensers, gyms etc. within their workplaces to help employees unwind.

11. Rationalising workload and time pressures

For ensuring proper balance between the professional and private lives of their employees, employers need to ensure that the workload on the former does not go beyond reasonable levels. Banking is perhaps one of the few jobs where even a small mistake or error could land an officer or clerk in big trouble. In some cases, the punishment could take the form of reimbursing the bank to the tune of lakhs or crores of rupees and in some others, it could mean loss of one's job itself, with a whole lot of other possibilities in between with regard to the nature of the punishment. And all this is apart from the traumatic experiences of the person concerned and his family for years on end, as a result of such events. In such situations, the average bank employee is always on edge. Similar experiences have worsened in recent times due to the relentless increase in the workload, including banks branching out into new areas like marketing of life insurance and non-life insurance products of other companies. No wonder then that an average employee returns home every day with toxic thoughts of unfinished work and unpleasant work experiences which in the long run, take a heavy toll on his health and well-being.

It must be remembered that every organisation emerges from the blood and sweat of their employees working at different levels of the hierarchy. Therefore, the least they deserve is care, concern and empathy from their organisations. And an organization which extends that care, concern and empathy to the employees is bound to do well in the marketplace as well. To buttress my point, I can do no better than quote the words of **Anne M. Mulcahy,** ***"Employees who believe that management is concerned about them as a whole person - not just an employee - are more productive, more satisfied, more fulfilled. Satisfied employees mean satisfied customers, which leads to profitability."***

CHAPTER 14

Performance Appraisal : Transparency Wins

"The task of leadership is to create an alignment of strengths...making a system's weaknesses irrelevant."
-Peter Drucker

When an organisation prepares balance sheet at periodical intervals, it takes into account the values of assets, liabilities, income and expenditure and other items which can be expressed in monetary terms. This means that the balance sheet speaks only of the quantifiable aspects of a business and excludes from its scope any assessment of the contributions made by the human resources of an organization. But, this should not lead us to any wrong conclusion. The quality of leadership available in a company, the motivation level of the workforce, their energy and enthusiasm levels, their sense of belonging to the company, their problem-solving skills etc. are of crucial importance to the productivity and development of an organization. But, as we know well, the aforesaid criteria are basically about intelligence, emotions, attitudes, temperament etc. which are not tangible and therefore, cannot be quantified in monetary terms. This is the reason why they do not find a place in the balance sheet of an organisation. Notwithstanding the aforesaid difficulty, any organization needs to have in place a suitable system of assessing the quality of its workforce for the purpose of taking decisions related to placement, promotion, training etc.

Performance appraisal

Personnel Management has basically two control mechanisms - one is periodical assessment of an employee's performance at work and the other is, administering the enforcement of discipline. This chapter is concerned only with the first part, namely, periodical assessment of job performance, also referred to as Performance appraisal. This exercise is normally carried out by the Human Resources Development Department of an organization. The first appraisal is done at the time of appointment of an employee. The subsequent appraisals carried out during the working life of an employee on an annual basis are used for assessing his suitability for promotions as also for taking placement and training related decisions. On the basis of the performance appraisals, the employees are classified into different grades e.g. Excellent, Average, Below Average, Poor.

Performance appraisal consists of the following steps:

a) Establishing and communicating performance standards
While designing each job and formulating the job description, the performance standards too should be laid down in clear, objective and measurable terms. Once the performance standards are set, they should be communicated to the employees in clear and objective terms. The employee should not have to guess what he has to do.

b) Measuring and comparing actual performance with standards
Measuring is a crucial stage of the performance evaluation process and it should be done only with regard to the jobs assigned to the employee. For this, personal observations, statistical reports, oral reports and written reports of various kinds are the sources relied upon by the superiors. Comparing process involves identifying the deviations noted in actual performance from the standards put in place.

c) Discussing the appraisal with the employee
This step involves communicating the result of the appraisal to the employee. Communicating a favourable appraisal rating is always easy while conveying a negative one is a tricky exercise. In most cases, employees at the receiving end of a negative appraisal are very likely going to feel de-motivated. Hence, the superior should discuss with the employee and listen to his part of the story also while trying to identify the reason for the shortfall in his performance and the corrective steps needed. He should convince him that one adverse appraisal does not in any way mean the end of the road for him as long as he is prepared to work to improve himself.

Judgmental errors during performance appraisal

There is a popular saying which goes like this- “A person often sees the world as he is, not as it is". As such, judgments made by human beings are often coloured by subjectivity and prone to inaccuracy and errors. A sincere and efficient worker may not be liked by many superiors if he is in the habit of speaking truth bluntly to their face. Similarly, a junior officer who has had a verbal clash with the Branch Manager may never be able to win the latter's affections. Then there are cases where the superior officer plays favourites based on the gender, skin colour, behavioural traits, religion etc. of employees. To sum up, given the inherent subjectivity involved in the performance appraisal exercise, the performance ratings may not in all cases pass the test of objectivity, equity and fairness. Therefore, the organisation must put in place a control mechanism to ensure that likes and dislikes of superiors, favouritism or bias of any kind are not allowed to influence the performance appraisal exercise.

FACTORS ADVERSELY IMPACTING PERFORMANCE APPRAISAL EXERCISE

Halo effect

Halo effect is a kind of cognitive bias in which our positive perception of one trait of a person tends to get extended to other aspects of the person's character and personality also. Thus, it is common to find physically attractive men or women being automatically thought of as being kind, intelligent and knowledgeable without any evidence to support this assumption. This is a common perceptual error generally observed while rating the performance of employees. Because of the superior's positive bias towards a single outstanding trait, any weakness or shortcoming of the individual under other criteria may not be perceived, thus defeating the purpose of the performance appraisal exercise. An employee working long hours in the office, though really incompetent, may be regarded as an efficient worker and given a better rating than he deserves.

Horns effect

The opposite of the Halo effect is the Horns effect. Here, our negative perception of a particular trait in a particular person gets extended to the assessment of the rest of his character and personality also. As a result, if a person is considered deficient in a particular trait, then that person is automatically assumed to be deficient in many other traits as well. For example, an employee who is occasionally a latecomer for valid reasons may also be assumed to be undisciplined or lazy by the superiors. Similarly, if an employee comes casually dressed up to office every day, he may get a negative rating not only under 'dressing' but also under other unconnected parameters.

The Similar-to-me bias

This bias is to be seen both at the workplace and the world outside. Young men tend to rate young men higher than older men under certain criteria while the older men tend to rate older men higher than younger men under the same criteria. Women tend to rate women higher than men under some criteria while men tend to rate men higher than women under the same criteria and so on. To sum up, similarity in anything, be it gender, age, race, mother tongue or ideology, often tends to lead to a certain kind of solidarity between the appraiser and the appraisee which may influence the appraisal.

Unwarranted leniency or strictness

Some superiors adopt a more lenient approach during the performance appraisal exercise and give favourable ratings to all their subordinates. Some others do just the opposite as they focus only on the shortcomings of their subordinates and give low ratings to all of them, rendering the whole exercise meaningless.

The Contrast effect

Some reporting officers tend to overuse comparison as a tool while rating their subordinates. For example, let's say, both officer 'A' and officer 'B' are good at handling correspondence with customers. But, the former shows a literary bent in his language while the latter's language is direct and business-like. If the branch manager loves literature, he may have a tendency to rate 'A' higher even if both kinds of writing are serving the purpose equally well.

Rating based exclusively on past or present performance

Sometimes, the present performance is evaluated based on the past track record or a past event. This is known as the spill-over effect. Sometimes, it is the reverse-rating may be influenced by the most recent behaviour of a subject or a most recent event involving him. Both these approaches run the risk of underestimating or overestimating an officer due to their focus on one period or one event.

Middle of the road approach

Some superiors rate all the employees as average performers, adopting a middle-of-the-road approach. This approach neither serves the best interests of the employees nor of the organisation. This play-safe model hides the truth of the real performance of the employees and as such, it defeats the very purpose of performance evaluation.

How to ensure objectivity and fairness in the performance appraisal exercise?

Submission of objective and correct data by the officer adhering to time schedule

In practice, many officers are very casual in submitting their annual self-appraisal to the reporting officer. The officer concerned should truthfully and correctly write whatever is asked for in the form. Some reporting officers too, adopt a casual and mechanical approach when it comes to assessing the performance of their subordinates. The tendency to commence the exercise at the eleventh hour indicates lack of seriousness on the part of the concerned towards this important task. It must be realised that performance evaluation exercise is closely linked to the performance of an organization.

The Performance appraisal reports should not be mechanically prepared and analyzed on the basis of data alone. An important thing to be noted here is that personal opinion of the reporting officer would have an important bearing while finalizing the report. Hence, some subjectivity is bound to be there in the final appraisal report. For instance, the competence of an officer under parameters like communication skills, leadership qualities and interpersonal skills, by and large, is assessed based on the subjective assessment made by the reporting officer. That said, the subjectivity manifested in the appraisal should neither be of the kind which consciously destroys the careers of subordinates nor the kind which acts as leverage to the undeserving candidates to get elevation to higher posts.

Transparency and feedback

Performance appraisal should not be reduced to fault-finding exercise. The ultimate purpose of the exercise is to improve the overall productivity and efficiency of the organization. The shortcomings in the performance, if any, can be communicated to the employee by way of feedback and this in turn, is expected to help him improve his job performance.

The performance appraisal report should not be treated as something super-secret like inquiry reports or charge-sheets. It deserves transparency as its overall aim should be motivational. There should be meaningful discussions on performance-related matters between the officer concerned and the reporting officer and it must be conducted in a cordial atmosphere. Any serious inadequacy in performance must be communicated to the employee before finalising the rating. The positive and the negative aspects of the appraisal must be discussed frankly and fearlessly. Ideally, both of them must agree with the final review. It is desirable to appreciate the appraisee's hardworking nature and other positive qualities also while being open about their shortcomings. The report should not be biased or envious to the extent of blocking the progress of even the honest and hardworking individuals who might have some minor flaws in their character but otherwise, have the potential to grow as valuable assets for the organization over time.

A reporting officer should be competent enough to counsel problematic employees and bring them on track in time. For this, a reporting officer should familiarise himself with the counselling techniques. He/she should not nurse any kind of prejudice, should display wisdom, maturity and be mindful of human dignity. He must also ensure that his functions and activities as reporting officer are always closely aligned with the super-ordinate goals of the organisation.

Performance appraisal: A tool for promotion

Usually, for promotion of an employee the information relating to educational qualification, experience, rating of performance appraisal, result of the interview and confidential reports, if any, are carefully considered. Generally, promotions to higher posts are given by organizations to deserving candidates only. The career growth of deserving employees is closely linked to the growth of an organization itself. If undeserving candidates without the required qualities are elevated, the organisational interest will be jeopardized and this will impact the growth and development of the organization. Therefore, the promotion process should be conducted with a high sense of professionalism, justice and fairness. There should be no room for discrimination, partiality, favouritism, conflict of interest etc. at any stage of the process. It must never be forgotten that for an employee the promotion process is a gateway to a higher position in the organization accompanied by increase in salary. A promotion also enhances his prestige and standing in the eyes of his peers and society in general. In return for these, the employee is expected to put his heart and soul into his work for the organization. In view of the aforesaid, merit and merit alone should be the only criterion for promotion.

Leadership vs Performance: Ground reality

Traditionally, Indian banks assign higher weightage to business performance while selecting candidates for promotion to higher positions. In contrast, some U.S. banks like Bank of America consider business performance as a matter of numbers only. These banks reportedly attach greater importance to leadership and inter-personal skills. Dale Carnegie in his book 'Leadership mastery' (Page nos. 62-63) has narrated the case of a senior vice-president of Bank of America who was fired from his job despite his outstanding record under business performance because he was weak in leadership skills.When the executive pointed to the good work he had done for Bank of America, his boss replied, 'People just don't want working with you. We are not looking for just performance as the performance is just a matter of numbers. You need leadership talent.'

The ability of a bank manager to secure business does not depend on his drive, initiative and dynamism alone, it also depends on a number of variables over which he has no control such as location of the branch, the demographic profile of the people living in the area, presence or absence of industrial and commercial units. For instance, if a bank branch is located in a residential area populated mostly by lower middle-class people with just a few retail shops to show for commercial activities, the branch manager may not be able to grow the business much despite all his excellent leadership and inter-personal skills. In such a case, to judge his performance entirely on the basis of business will be unfair. This is not to cast any aspersions on the leadership and inter-personal skills of branch managers and officers who have toiled and canvassed sizeable business for a bank, but to highlight the need for a holistic judgment on the performance competencies of an officer before he is promoted.

Employees should seize the opportunity to display their talents

Recognising and rewarding talent through promotions or otherwise is no doubt the responsibility of the organization. But, an officer too has a responsibility in this regard. If he has talent, commitment, communication ability and a track record of good interpersonal relations, he should let his superiors and colleagues know about it instead of remaining passive and complacent. The superiors, on their part, must create an enabling environment for the staff members and allow them unfettered freedom to unleash their innovative skills and creativity for the good of the organization. As Benjamin West, the famous painter, has rightly said, "*To recognize great talent, we must encourage dreamers.*"

PERFORMANCE APPRAISAL IN PSBs - A WELCOME DEVELOPMENT

Till 2019, in the public sector banks, only the performance of the head of a branch was assessed in a budgetary format (showing quantifiable targets) whereas the performance of other officers working in a branch was assessed in a non-budgetary format (not showing quantifiable targets). In the case of administrative offices too, the same situation existed. The performance of the head of an administrative office would be assessed in budgetary format (showing quantifiable targets), while the assessment of performance of other officers working in the administrative offices would be made in the non-budgetary format (not showing quantifiable targets). As a result of this, the entire responsibility of achieving the targets rested solely on the shoulders of the heads of branches/ROs/COs/RRBs which was quite unfair to the officials holding these positions. In view of the aforesaid, in 2019, as part of the PSB Reforms Agenda, Public Sector Banks brought in major reforms in their system of performance appraisal with respect to officer employees working in branches and administrative units. The gist of these reforms is given below:

1. The performance of all eligible officers working in branches is to be assessed under the budgetary format as in the case of Branch Heads. For this purpose, Key Responsibility Areas (KRAs) are to be identified by the reporting officer based on the duties entrusted to the officers and financial or non-financial targets, as the case may be, are to be allotted to them under each KRA. The officers are to be apportioned monthly targets based on the yearly targets and assessed on a quarterly-weighted basis.

2. As against the earlier practice, officers working in administrative/ service units too are to be assessed under the budgetary format. The Key Responsibility Areas of these officers are to be identified by the reporting officers concerned and then suitable targets are allotted to them under each KRA. An indicative list of KRA-based targets is given below:

a. Number of recovery camps conducted
b. Number of NPA parties contacted for recovery
c. Number of parties referred for loan accounts
d. Number of parties referred for issuance of credit cards
e. Number of inspection reports closed within time norms
f. Number of credit reports reviewed with time norms
g. Number of credit proposals processed within time norms

These reforms considerably relieve the pressure on the branch heads and the administrative offices and ensure active participation of other officers in achieving the organizational objectives.

CHAPTER 15

The Fight Against Money Laundering : An Explainer

By G G Menon
Staff Training College, Ernakulam
(Former Chief Manager and Principal, Staff Training College of erstwhile Syndicate Bank, now merged with Canara bank)

Harishankar was into the world of crime. His criminal activities ranged from drug peddling to arms smuggling to extortion. He wanted to launder a few crores of rupees he had earned through his illegal dealings. He approached Bank A's Surat branch to open a Current account in the name of M/s Golden Cosmetics. He informed the Branch Manager that he was the proprietor of the aforesaid firm which was in the business of manufacturing and selling perfumes. He wanted to deposit Rs.20 lakhs as initial deposit into the account and assured the Branch Manager that more such amounts would be deposited into the account from time to time. He duly produced his Aadhar card and his latest landline Telephone bill to satisfy the Branch Manager about his identity and address. The Branch Manager saw the visit of Harishankar as a godsend as the deposits of the branch were dwindling day by day, inviting caustic remarks from the Region head. He readily agreed to open the account and himself introduced Harishankar. Thereafter, there were regular deposits into the account with a daily minimum of Rs.1 lakhs. A few days later, Harishankar got some of his associates also to open Current accounts at the same branch of Bank A and three other branches located within Surat. He personally accompanied each associate at the time of opening the latter's account and introduced him to the Branch Manager as a supplier of raw materials for his perfumery. During the next few months, a number of transfers of funds were made from the account of M/s Golden Cosmetics to the accounts of the various associates and vice versa. And then, one day, almost the entire balance of about Rs. 4 crores lying in the account of M/s Golden Cosmetics was withdrawn and invested in a prime property in Baroda. Harishankar then floated a real estate firm under the name of ‘Hariom Real Estate’ based in Baroda which sold prime residential plots in Baroda city. He went to the Baroda main branch of Bank B to open a Current account in the name of the firm, M/s Hariom Real Estate posing as the Proprietor of the firm. Here too, Harishankar dangled the carrot of many lakhs of rupees of low-cost funds coming into the account in the days ahead. The Branch Manager was more than happy to facilitate matters for Harishankar. After opening of the account, the first thing Harishankar did was to start selling plot by plot, the prime property he had acquired earlier. The sale proceeds were duly deposited into the account of M/s Hariom Real Estate. By selling all the plots, Harishankar was able to make a total profit of about Rs.2 crores. Harishankar was very happy. But, the happiness was less about the profit booked and more about adding one more layer to the laundering process involving his money which had originated from various crimes.

What is money laundering?

The term “Money Laundering” is said to have originated from the Mafia* ownership of laundries in the United States. At one time during the 20th century, the Mafia gangs operating in the U.S. were earning huge sums of money in cash from crimes like extortion, prostitution, gambling, sale of illicit liquor etc. In order to give a legitimate cover for such tainted money, the Mafia groups started investing heavily in laundry businesses which gave birth to the expression “Money Laundering”. Money laundering is the process by which criminals attempt to hide and disguise the true origin and ownership of the proceeds from their criminal activities, thereby avoiding prosecution, conviction and confiscation of such funds. Since then, this criminal practice has spread far and wide. So much so that today it threatens peace, stability and prosperity in many societies across the globe. Money laundering is a problem that India too has been facing for many years. To fight the menace of Money laundering, India enacted the Prevention of Money Laundering Act in 2002. The Act has undergone amendments in 2005, 2009, 2012, 2015, 2019 and 2023. As per this Act as amended from time to time, "whosoever directly or indirectly attempts to indulge or knowingly assists or knowingly is a party or is actually involved in any process or activity connected with the proceeds of crime including its concealment, possession, acquisition or use and projecting or claiming it as untainted property shall be guilty of the offence of Money-laundering."

As can be seen from the above, as per the extant provisions under PMLA, 2002, the term Money laundering denotes the whole range of activities linked to Money laundering.

It is worth stressing here that even if an account was opened by a banker in good faith and without negligence, evidence of money laundering in the account, is sufficient to bring charges against the account holder, the banker, the introducer etc. under the AML Act, 2002. The banker could be charged with the crime of having knowingly assisted money laundering operation. The onus of proving that he did not knowingly do so would fall on the banker under the Act.

A point to note here is that the provisions of PML Act, 2002 cannot be invoked unless the money laundered relates to a scheduled offence under the said Act. The scheduled offences, also known as Predicate offences are those which have come from violations of the Acts listed in the Schedule to the PML Act, 2002. The Schedule to the PML Act, 2002 consists of three parts- Part A, Part B & Part C.

*A secret international organization of criminals mostly active in the U.S. and Italy.

Part A:
This part of the schedule lists offences under various Acts such as Indian Penal Code (IPC), 1860, Narcotic Drugs and Psychotropic Substances Act, 1985, Explosive Substances Act, 1908, Unlawful Activities (Prevention) Act (UAPA), 1967, Arms Act, 1959, Wildlife Protection Act, 1972, Immoral Traffic (Prevention) Act 1986, Prevention of Corruption Act, 1988 and so on. These offences, if followed by laundering of the related proceeds, will attract the provisions of the PML Act. The total number of Acts listed in the Schedule is currently 28. No value criteria of any kind are specified for the offences listed in this part of the Schedule.

Part B:
This part covers offences under the Acts listed under Part A where the value involved is Rs.1 crore or above. (This part was removed under the

amendment made to the Act in 2012).

Part C:
This part deals with offences involving cross-border crimes.

Many people have the misconception that Money laundering is resorted to only by people who want to evade income tax. Money laundering is a much wider issue. Money launderers may not have an issue with regard to paying tax on their ill-gotten money. Their problem is different and that is: The money they have got has come from an illegal source and they would like to make it appear that the money has come from a legal source. Interestingly, offences under the Income Tax Act, 1961 are not listed among the Scheduled offences under PML Act, 2002. The rationale for this is anybody's guess.

The provisions of the Anti-Money Laundering Act, 2002 are administered by the Enforcement Directorate. Persons found guilty of the offence of Money Laundering are liable for imprisonment for a term not less than 3 years and a fine up to Rs. 5 lakh. Where the offence was committed under the Narcotic and Psychotropic Substances Act, 1985, the imprisonment could extend up to 7 years. In addition to the aforesaid, the property/ies obtained by committing the scheduled offence are liable to be attached/ confiscated/disposed of as per orders of the Court concerned.

To develop a co-ordinated international response to the problem of money laundering, the Financial Action Task Force on money laundering was established by G-7 countries in 1989 as per a decision taken during the group's summit held in Paris in 1989. One of the first tasks of the FATF was to come out with recommendations which set out the measures national governments should take to implement effective anti-money laundering programmes. These measures are already in place in most countries.

Steps in Money Laundering

The basic Money Laundering process has the following three stages.

1. *Placement:* At this stage, the launderer places the tainted money with a legitimate financial institution. The money deposited is normally in the form of cash. For the money launderer, this is the most crucial stage of the operation as money deposited into an account in large amounts become conspicuous and also, banks are required to report them to the regulatory authorities. The launderer has to find ways and means to overcome these hurdles.
2. *Layering:* Layering is the process of creating a maze of transactions around the original transaction with a view to giving a legitimate appearance to the funds and making the audit trail as difficult as possible for any investigator. Layering may consist of several bank-to-bank transfers, wire transfers between different accounts in different names in different countries, making deposits and withdrawals to continually vary the amount of money in the accounts, changing the money's currency, buying high-value items like boats, houses, cars, diamonds etc. to change the form of the money and so on.
3. *Integration:* At the integration stage, the money re-enters the mainstream economy after assuming a legitimate-looking form i.e. it appears to have come from a legal source. This may involve one or more bank transfers into the account of a local business in which the launderer has planned to invest.

Going back to the example cited earlier, Harishankar did not actually run any business in cosmetics as claimed by him when he approached Bank A to open the Current account in the name of M/s Golden Cosmetics. His sole purpose in opening the account was to launder his ill-gotten money by inserting it into the banking system. The bank opened the account and allowed operations in it without even confirming that the business really existed. This was the **Placement stage** of the money laundering operation. The opening of the accounts of Harishankar's associates with the same bank branch and others in the city; the subsequent money transfers from the firm's account to the associates' accounts and vice versa and the closure of the account and investment of the entire balance in a prime property located in Baroda were all part of a clever plan to muddy the waters as much as possible so as to make any future investigation into the source of the money as difficult as possible. This was the **Layering stage.** Harishankar setting up a new real-estate firm under the name of Hariom Real Estate and depositing the sale proceeds of the residential plots into that firm's account constituted the next and last stage of the operation where the ill-gotten money acquires a legitimate appearance and re-enters the mainstream economy. This is called the **Integration stage**.

Money laundering-Modus operandi

Methods to launder money have been evolving rapidly in recent years in response to heightened anti-money laundering measures taken by national governments. Today, very sophisticated methods are used to move illicit money through financial systems across the globe. The following are some of the more commonly used methods used to launder money.

1. Structuring deposits or Smurfing: Money launderers are always careful about not drawing the least attention to what they do. For example, let's suppose a person has crores of illicit money stashed abroad in an offshore account and wants to bring it to India to launder and then invest in a legitimate business. He will make arrangements to remit amounts to be decided by him, (not large enough to draw attention of the regulatory authorities) to tens or hundreds of accounts in India from his offshore account. Of course, this would be done with the consent of the account holders and may involve payment of incentives to them considering the risk involved. After this part of the operation is completed, the individuals who received the remittances in their accounts would be asked at a suitable time to remit the respective amounts to the specified account of the launderer in India. To receive the remittances, the money launderer would in the meanwhile set up a legitimate business in India and open a bank account in its name to blend his existing and future ill-gotten money with the legitimate money generated by the business. Of course, all this cannot happen without the connivance of bank managers, chartered accountants etc. The process described above is called structuring or smurfing,

2. Shell companies: These are companies that are created for no other reason than to help launder illegitimate money. They are to be found mostly in 'Tax haven' countries like Bermuda, the Bahamas, the British Virgin islands, the Cayman Islands etc. The shell companies normally do no business. They exist only on paper. The shell companies receive the 'dirty' money from the money launderer in their bank account and create legitimate-looking business transactions in the account from time to time to give the appearance of running a business. To support this, they also create fake invoices, fake balance sheet etc. Of course, all this is done only for an exorbitant fee. The proceeds lying in the account could be used for financing the launderer's expenses while on visits abroad, his children's education abroad, for buying foreign assets, investing in Indian companies through a process called round-tripping etc.

3. Investing in legitimate businesses: Money launderers like to invest in large businesses like brokerage firms or casinos that deal with big volumes of money or cash intensive businesses like bars, car washes, laundry etc. The reason for this is that in such businesses, it becomes easier for the money launderer to blend the dirty money with legitimate money and conceal the true origin of the former from the regulatory bodies.

4. Purchasing lottery tickets of winners: Money launderers normally keep track of the winners of various lotteries conducted within the country. The winners are persuaded to hand over the lottery ticket to the money launderer and in return, they are paid the prize money or more. Most winners fall for the offer as this way they can avoid paying income tax which otherwise, they would have to pay.

5. Under-invoicing exports and Over-invoicing imports: Money launderers directly or through their accomplices often resort to this method to launder their illicit money. When export is under-invoiced, the value shown in the invoice would be less than the actual value of the goods. When the bill is received abroad, the importer (Buyer) would pay the full invoice value to the collecting bank. The difference between the actual value and the invoice value would be remitted by him to the offshore account of the seller as per prior understanding between the two parties. In the case of imports, money laundering can be done by over-invoicing the imported goods, which means that the invoice value will be more than the actual value. In this case, as per prior understanding, after the import bill is paid by the Indian importer (Buyer), the overseas exporter (Seller) retains the actual value of the goods only and remits the difference between the actual value and the invoice value to the specified offshore account of the Buyer.

The above items are only illustrative. There are many more methods of money laundering to discuss. But, due to constraints of space, that will have to wait until another day.

Effects of money laundering

Money laundering helps criminals to not only escape punishment for their heinous deeds but also enjoy a life of leisure and luxury. No civil society can afford to allow this. Further, the laundered money is often reinvested to commit more criminal acts including human trafficking, prostitution, financing of terrorism etc., leading to death and destruction, law and order problems and misery to millions of people.

Massive influx of illicit money into particular sectors of the economy attractive to money launderers because of various reasons e.g. construction, bars, casinos, creates false demand in such sectors. Seeing this, the government may adjust its economic policy to facilitate more investment in these sectors. As a result, more illicit money may flow into these sectors. However, at some point, the enforcement officials may get wind of the real reason for the boom i.e. money laundering, and start investigating. At that point, all the illicit monies invested in these businesses for laundering may start disappearing leading to closure of businesses and unemployment of thousands of people. Money laundering can also cause serious distortions to a country's imports and exports. For example, on the import side, criminal elements often use illicit money to purchase luxury goods made abroad for using them or as part of the process of laundering illicit funds. Such imports do not generate any economy or employment. In fact, large-scale imports of such items can depress the prices of similar products made domestically and reduce the profitability of the manufacturing units concerned. For banks in general, any association with money laundering, knowingly or otherwise, is fraught with disastrous consequences as such banks could become the subject of investigation by law enforcement agencies with the attendant reputational risk and the possibility of their assets being frozen.

Conclusion: As most of the money laundering takes place through banking channels, the importance of strict compliance of KYC norms can hardly be overstated. It may be mentioned here that following the said norms does not end with obtaining proof of identity and address from the customer at the time of opening his/her account. Every branch is also expected to make a thorough enquiry into the business/profession of the account holder in order to verify the information furnished in this regard, prepare his/her risk profile based on the relevant parameters, put in place monitoring measures applicable to the risk category of the account and report transactions in the account, wherever required, to FIU-IND.

All things considered, money laundering is a serious threat to peace, prosperity and stability across most of the globe. Not just national governments but also every individual citizen should join the fight against this threat. One would like to conclude with the following words of Cecilia Malmstrom, former Home Affairs Commissioner, European Union which might as well act as the roadmap for all countries of the world in their fight against money laundering. ***"Dirty money has no place in our economy, whether it comes from drug deals, the illegal guns trade or trafficking in human beings. We must make sure that organized crime cannot launder its funds through the banking system or the gambling sector. Our banks should never function as laundromats for mafia money, or enable the funding of terrorists".***

CHAPTER 16

The Transformational Saga Of South Indian Bank

"A leader is one who sees more than others see, who sees farther than others see and who sees before others see."
-LeRoy Eims

South Indian Bank is one of the oldest banks in Kerala. It was incorporated as a private limited company in Thrissur under the name of "The South Indian Bank Limited" on Jan. 29, 1929. A brainchild of a group of enterprising men, the bank was established to encourage the habit of thrift among the public by acting as a safe, efficient and professional repository for their hard-earned money and to make life easier for businessmen in general by providing credit to them at reasonable rates of interest, thus freeing them from the clutches of usurious moneylenders. In 1939, it became a public limited company. In 1946, SIB became the first private bank in Kerala to receive the status of a scheduled bank under the RBI Act. Over the years, the bank was able to grow its business slowly and steadily which was partly helped by the takeover of certain smaller banks at different points of time. Till the early years of the new millennium, the bank's operations had been confined mainly to the state of Kerala with a modest presence in some of the other southern states. The public image of the bank was that of a staid, traditional, conservative and risk-averse bank which had little appetite for anything new or novel. But, all this was to change after a gentleman named Dr. V.A. Joseph joined the bank as its Chairman & CEO in 2005. While continuing in that post, he was redesignated as Managing Director & CEO of the bank in 2008.

Dr. Joseph came to SIB after his decades-long innings with Syndicate Bank, a leading public sector bank which was credited with pioneering a number of innovative products and services especially designed for the common man and the priority sector. These were later copied across the industry under various names. Starting as a probationary officer, Dr. Joseph worked in a variety of positions over the years and went on to head a number of branches, divisions and zones of Syndicate Bank before he was elevated to the post of General Manager. He had impeccable academic credentials which included a doctorate in personnel management, a post-graduate degree in commerce and personnel management and a law degree. He was also a Certified Associate of the Indian Institute of Bankers. Besides his mastery in various areas of banking, he possessed an analytical bent of mind, a keen eye for detail and deep insights into the working of the human psyche in the organizational context. All this helped him to turn in consistently good performances regardless of the post he held or the office he worked in. It may be mentioned here that among the posts held by Dr. Joseph in Syndicate Bank was that of Personnel Manager (Human Resources) at the bank's head office in Manipal. This enabled him to further hone his specialised skills in the area of personnel management. This experience was to stand him in good stead later while dealing with the challenges that awaited him at South Indian Bank.

To start with, he formed a team consisting of some dynamic top executives under his leadership which was tasked with the responsibility of putting the bank back on the path of rapid progress after years of low or moderate growth. There was complete transparency within the team. Dr. Joseph made it clear to the team that he expected every member to actively participate during the brainstorming sessions and thereafter, in order to make the entire process a success any member who had an idea could present it before the team without any prior screening. The selection of ideas for execution was done only after all the presentations had been made and evaluated by the team. The selected ideas were then carried to their logical conclusion by the respective departments at the bank's head office. Matters which required consultations with the award staff, officers or their respective unions/associations before execution were taken up with them in right earnest and with complete transparency. As a result of the foregoing exercises painstakingly carried out over many months, Dr. Joseph and his team now had a clear idea of the various factors which were acting as constraints on SIB realising its full potential as one of the oldest banks in Kerala and the steps to be taken to overcome them. These constraints and how they were overcome during the period 2005-2014 make for a fascinating case study on how to turn around a bank where growth has slipped into a state of stasis or continuous low growth. In the following paragraphs, we will be discussing the interesting journey of Dr. Joseph and his team in detail.

THE CONSTRAINTS AND HOW THEY WERE OVERCOME

1. Changing the public perception about the bank

As mentioned above, in 1946, SIB became the first private bank in Kerala to be classified as a Scheduled Bank. In the year, 2004, it completed 75 years of its existence. Most of Its branches were already computerised and were operating on the automated and sophisticated Finacle core banking software platform. The bank was able to offer products and services which could match the best offered by any other bank, public or private. Yet, the growth recorded by the bank since its birth was nothing much to write home about even after 75 years. As for the public image of the bank, it was widely perceived as a staid, conservative, traditional and risk-averse bank. This perception about the bank was stronger among the younger generation of bank customers. In fact, in the northern parts of the country, many people harboured the mistaken notion that South Indian Bank was a co-operative bank dealing mostly with gold loans.

Dr. Joseph and his team set about addressing the image issue first. After extensive discussions with the top management team and interactions with employees across the bank, it was decided to adopt a new logo and a new tagline for the bank which would boldly and attractively present before the public the new modern, dynamic and vibrant culture of the bank. As expected, the idea did not receive unanimous support from all. Many a doubting Thomas found no merit in the idea. For instance, a few senior employees were apprehensive that the change would not go down well with the older generation of the bank's customers and would cost the bank heavily. Dr. Joseph would listen to such views respectfully and respond disarmingly thus: "Put the blame squarely on me if it fails but take the entire credit if it succeeds". On October 16, 2006, the new logo with the new tagline was unveiled by Mammooty, the handsome and suave Malayalam cine star, a winner of multiple national awards for his enormous acting talent who also enjoyed a phenomenal fan following. The star had already been made the brand ambassador of the bank. It will not be out of place to mention here that SIB was the first among the old generation banks to appoint a brand ambassador to represent its brand. The new logo showed two hands strongly clasping a pillar symbolised by the acronym "SIB". Set in cardinal red and white colours representing energy, creativity and warmth, the new logo effusing vibrancy and vitality truly encapsulated the new approach of the bank. Visually, the clasping hands were also suggestive of a stylised 'S' representing service, strength, smartness, support and safety. And below the symbol was the punchy tagline targeted at the new generation which read "Experience Next Generation Banking". The idea of a new logo and a new tagline was to prove a masterstroke later. It not only made the public aware of the bank's evolution from a traditional and conservative bank to one where tradition and technology got blended to offer customers the best of both worlds but also had a positive effect on the morale of the workforce.

2. Addressing low morale of employees & reviving sense of belonging and organizational pride

Another major factor constraining the growth of the bank was the rather low morale of the employees in general and the lack of the required sense of belonging and organizational pride in them. The makeover given to the bank's image by the new logo and the brand ambassador had of course addressed the issue to some extent. But, much more remained to be done. After careful analysis of the extant HR policies and the related data, Dr. Joseph was able to put his finger on the main reasons for the above state of affairs. The first one was of course the limited scope for career progression available to employees. Another matter which was the cause of much employee dissatisfaction was the policy of posting even members of the Award staff i.e. Clerks and Sub-staff, outside their home state. Being simpler to sort out, Dr. Joseph chose to address the second issue first. He stopped the practice of posting Clerks and Sub-staff outside their home states. By removing a major irritant, Dr. Joseph was able to win overnight the hearts and support of the employees at the lower ranks who were the public face of the bank.

Soon Dr.Joseph and his team came out with a revamped fast track promotion policy for employees. The policy struck a fine balance between merit on the one hand and seniority on the other, thus ensuring a win-win situation for all concerned.

As a former personnel manager, Dr. Joseph was well aware of the importance of rewards and recognition in getting the best out of employees. After a number of brainstorming sessions with his team, Dr. Joseph came out with a bouquet of incentives to reward the performers in the bank irrespective of their post and rank. One of the incentives offered was a return trip to a foreign destination for the "top performers" and their spouses at the bank's cost. It may be mentioned here that the bank was among the earliest in the industry to introduce a performance-linked system of incentives over and above the pay. Additionally, it was also decided to prominently display the names of every achiever in SIB's role of honour. The bank's incentivizing initiatives would reach an altogether different level in 2009 when it introduced the Employees' stock option scheme which offered to all the employees the option of becoming a shareholder of the bank.

It may be mentioned here that the performance-linked system of incentives and the Employees' stock option scheme were introduced in the bank long before they found a place in the 11th bipartite settlement covering the pay and other terms and conditions applicable to bank employees. These are just two examples of how the decision-making process at the bank in general was characterized by a futuristic vision and clarity of thought.

3. Making employees feel that they count and fostering team spirit

For any organization to achieve success, it is necessary that the employees not only have a proud sense of belonging to it but also feel important about themselves and the work they do. Alongside, team spirit among the employees too needs to be fostered. To this end, annual family meets were conducted at various centres, to which the spouses and the children of the employees were also invited. The MD and CEO regularly attended such programmes. The idea behind holding such meets was to not just recognise the outstanding contributions of various staff members but also, acknowledge and appreciate the support extended to them by their family members in this regard. It was also a way of telling the families of the employees that they too were partners in the progress of the bank and thus establishing an emotional connect with them. The bank also started inviting and hosting eminent personalities drawn from various walks of life for interacting and sharing space with staff members thus giving an opportunity to the latter to hear first-hand about the inspiring journeys of some great and iconic Indians.

The bank's continuing concern for the welfare of its employees and their families was in evidence again when it introduced the 4-year long sabbatical scheme for women employees to enable them to do justice to their role as homemakers. Further, in order to provide succour to families of employees dying in harness, the bank introduced a scheme for offering compassionate employment under which one member of the deceased employee's family would be eligible for a job matching his/her educational qualification, skills and experience.

Besides the above, arrangements were made to ensure that all employees were kept in the loop as regards important banking-related developments within and outside the bank using technological tools. It may be mentioned here that nearly 75 to 80% of the bank's operations had already been computerised by the year 2004-05.

4. Improving the age profile of the bank

Another constraint on growth identified by Dr. Joseph and his team was the average age profile of the employees which was above 50 years. Though there was no definite scientific data to establish any correlation between ageing and productivity, empirical evidence did seem to suggest that aging adversely affects a human being's capacity to work in a sustained and focussed way for long periods of time. Besides this, there was another angle to aging. Around the ages of 50-55 years, the breadwinner in a typical Indian family has to start worrying about a number of new issues outside his official responsibilities like financing and ensuring completion of children's higher education, conducting marriage of daughter, addressing health issues of self and family etc. In the case of some employees, these can become major distractions with the potential to affect their productivity adversely.

Many of the older employees had just 3-4 years of service left. The only reason for their continuing in the job seemed to be the absence any other option before them. Dr. Joseph and his team had a gut feeling that many of them would be willing to opt for voluntary retirement, provided it came as part of an attractive package which *inter alia* could cushion them against any hardship resulting from the voluntary premature retirement. There was complete unanimity among the team members that a suitable VRS was a good idea to try out for improving the age profile of the workforce. Therefore, Dr. Joseph and his team now focused their attention and energies on designing a suitable Voluntary Retirement Scheme for all the employees desirous of prematurely quitting their jobs. Finally, the bank came out with a very liberal Voluntary Retirement Scheme for eligible employees on attractive terms which included the offer of a suitable job to any one eligible member of the retiring employee's family.

The scheme received overwhelming response. So much so that after the eligible VRS applicants were relieved from their jobs, the average age of employees dropped from over 50 years to 34 years! The bank followed this up by recruiting new hands for different positions. All of them were young and well-educated, some of them holding B.Tech and even M.Tech degrees. Their motivation levels and mobility too were high. And to top it all, these new recruits were all starting at the lowest point of their respective scales which helped the bank make substantial savings under the head 'Salaries'. The major gains from the VRS were a younger workforce, improved per employee productivity, improved customer service, substantial reduction in salary expenditure and improved profitability.

5. Increasing the number and geographical spread of branches

The bank was born in the year 1929. By 2004, it had completed 75 years. Yet, it was basically a bank confined to southern India. Its presence north of the Vindhyas was negligible which perhaps explains the funny though wrong notion then prevailing in many parts of northern India about the bank being a co-operative bank which handled only gold loans. Besides, the number of branches which stood at 450 was too small for a bank which was already 75 years old. It was also becoming obvious to the bank's top management that the bank was losing out on a lot of potential business by not opening branches in other parts of India where industries, trade and commerce were booming. In the light of this, the bank embarked on a large-scale expansion of its branch network by opening branches in various towns and cities with large business potential. In the year 2004-2005 alone, 69 new branches were opened, most of them in the northern parts of the country. To meet the requirement of staff for these branches, the management recruited local aspirants for various jobs. This served two purposes. First, it minimised the disruptions due to transfers which is the case when staff from other states are posted in branches and secondly, it went a long way to meet the demand for jobs to sons-of-the-soil which was increasingly being voiced by many political and other outfits across India. Of course, with the opening of the new branches, some senior and experienced employees had to be moved out from their home states as the new branches could not be left entirely in the hands of the new recruits. The unions expectedly resisted this move with full force. To dispel their apprehensions, the management came out with a new pro-employee transfer policy which *inter alia* provided for the transfer of such displaced employees back to their home states as soon as vacancies arose.

6. Recruitment and training of manpower

As Dr. Joseph and his team had envisioned, the bank had now entered a new phase where it was growing in more ways than one. Its geographical reach and network was growing; its business was growing and the range of activities it was handling too was growing. A new atmosphere of enthusiasm, adventure and boundless energy pervaded the bank. Dr. Joseph realised that this phase in the bank's journey could proceed smoothly and successfully, only if it had the right kind of manpower. With this in mind, a bold decision was taken by the management to shift the search for manpower from the open market to campuses. The campuses selected covered a variety of disciplines as a growing bank like SIB needed talents of various hues. The success of this new policy can be judged from the following break-up figures of employees with higher qualifications among the total workforce,

Total number of employees 7111

Out of which,

Management graduates	1170
Post-graduates	976
Engineers	647
Law graduates	90
Chartered accountants	91
Cost accountants	51
PhDs	2

With his deep insights into various facets of HR management, Dr. Joseph understood very well that along with educational qualifications employees needed to have the right attitude, aptitude and skills for extending professional, prompt and courteous service to the customers. With this in mind, new staff training colleges were set up in Mumbai, Bangalore, Coimbatore and Chennai. The training syllabus was comprehensive and covered the entire gamut of banking operations. During 2013-14, the bank imparted training to 2647 Officers, 1200 clerks and 53 Sub-staff on various aspects of banking operations. With this, cumulatively 55% of the 7000+ employees of the bank stood thoroughly trained.

7. Efficient NPA management

In recent years, NPAs have emerged as an existential threat to the banking sector. SIB too had its share of NPAs though they never reached dangerous levels due to a well-planned policy to prevent/manage NPAs. Under this policy, branches were required to continuously monitor each loan account from day one and initiate necessary follow-up action at the slightest sign of mismanagement or sickness. Thereafter, branches were required to adopt a two-pronged approach of "persuasion, wherever possible and permissible coercion, wherever necessary". This policy paid rich dividends to the bank as evidenced by the fact that the percentage of net NPAs to net advances which was 3.81% during 2004-2005 came down to 0.78% by 2013-2014.

What did the transformation achieve?

In the foregoing paragraphs, we have discussed at length the challenges before Dr. Joseph after he joined SIB in 2005 as Chairman & CEO and the strategies he employed to overcome them. At this stage, readers will be naturally curious to know whether all the elaborate planning and strategising by Dr. Joseph and his team followed by some decisive actions on the ground, produce the desired outcomes. After all, as the cliché goes, the proof of the pudding is in the eating. This writer would like to answer that in just a few sentences.

It would be an understatement to say that Dr. Joseph and his team achieved what they set out to achieve. It was much more than that. The strategies planned and executed by Dr. Joseph and his team met with resounding success of a kind which has few parallels in the history of Indian banking. This success not only lifted SIB out of the morass of low growth it had slipped into over the years but also catapulted it into a high-growth trajectory from where there has been no looking back for the bank. The following comparative data for 2005-06 and 2013-14 and the list of awards won by the bank appearing thereafter speak for themselves. **

	2005-2006	**2013-2014**
Number of branches	450	802
Total deposits of the bank	Rs. 9,578 cr.	Rs.47,491 Cr
Total loans and advances of the bank	Rs.6,370 cr.	Rs. 36,403 cr.
Total profit of the bank	Rs.50.90 cr.	Rs.507 cr.

***Dr. Joseph joined the bank as Chairman & CEO in 2005-2006 and his tenure with the bank ended in 2013-14 when he was MD & CEO of the bank.*

RECOGNITION GALORE

2014 - IDRBT Technology Excellence Award
2014 - IBA Technology Excellence Award
2013 - Sunday Standard Best Banker Award
2013 - MasterCard Innovation Award
2011 - D&B Best Bank - Asset Quality
2010 - Businessworld Best Bank Award
2009 - Financial Express Best Bank Award

The hard work and dynamism of Dr. Joseph who scripted the above success story still inspire his successors and its splendid legacy as a frontline successful old generation private sector bank, with its enduring new image of *'a new generation bank'* continues......

Having traced the inspiring story of Dr. Joseph and his team from its beginning to its successful denouement, it is time to conclude. And what better way to conclude than narrating the following conversation between Dr. Joseph and this writer some years ago?

We were seated on the lawn of a hotel. We had been talking for about an hour. It was time to end the conversation. It was then that this writer thought of asking Dr. Joseph one last question. The question was, whether the astounding outcomes from the transformational work done by him and his team had really been expected when the whole project started. In response, Dr. Joseph grinned and said that while handling such assignments, it is important that planning is far-sighted and meticulous and execution perfect; and if these two aspects are well taken care of, that would be half the battle won. The remaining half consists of many imponderables over which you have little control. He added that he and his team managed to get both the planning and the execution aspects right. And then, with a twinkle in his eyes, he pointed his right index finger skyward and said, "As for outcomes, remember that they are decided up there. All that you can do is to keep your fingers crossed and hope for the best." One could not agree more with him.

"If your actions inspire others to dream more, learn more, do more and become more, you are a leader."
-John Quincy Adams

Annexure - 1

Chandrasekharan. V, *Life Lessons for All Seasons*

Covey, Sean *The Seven Habits of Highly Effective Teens*

Covey, Stephen *8th Habit* : *From effectiveness to greatness*

Covey, Stephen *Principle Centred Leadership*

Covey, Stephen *Seven Habits of Highly Effective People*

Das M.K and Dr Thomas E.M, *A Southern Odyssey, The Story of South Indian Bank*

Drucker, Peter *The effective executive, Butterworth-Heinemann*

Ghosh, Biswanath Personnel Management and Industrial Relations - Its theory and practice in India (Published by World Press, Kolkata)

Henry, Todd *Die Empty, Unleash Your Best Work Every Day*

Indian Institute of Banking and Finance, Macmillan Publishers India Limited *Human Resources Management*

John W. Newstrom and Keith Davis *Organisation Behaviour- Human Behaviour at work* (Published by Tata McGraw Hill)

Kramer, Paul, Fighting Body Pollution - Staying healthy in an healthy world

Luthans, Fred *Organisation Behaviour*

Peck, Scott, *The Road Less Travelled*

Reader's Digest, *Write Better Speak Better*

Toffler, Alvin *Future Shock*

Toffler, Alvin *Powershift*

Annexure - 2

LEADERSHIP EXCELLENCE, THE TAJ WAY

On November 26, 2008, the Taj Mahal Palace hotel in Mumbai witnessed an unprecedented terrorist operation. The whole night witnessed terrorists rampaging through the hotel, hurling grenades and firing automatic weapons. The employees displayed extraordinary valour and dedication to duty, risking their lives. The employees were calmly active and helped the trapped people escape quickly. While evacuating 1,500 guests to escape, 11 employees laid down their lives. It is the customer-centric culture of the Taj Hotel employees which prompted them to safeguard the guests in times of life-threatening situation. In the terrorist rampaging episode, altogether 31 people reportedly died and 28 were hurt. This in brief was what had happened on those cursed moments of that day.

ORDINARY HEROES DISPLAYS EXTRAORDINARY VALOUR – FACTS AND INFERENCE

The unique features of recruitment: The incredible sense of customer centricity, amidst the life-threatening situation, owes to the value driven recruitment system in vogue in the Taj hotels. Their employees who hold Indian values like respect for elders, humility, consideration, discipline, and honesty were recruited from the small towns and not from metro cities. They were mostly from high schools located in small towns and semi-urban areas and they were so emotionally connected to the company and empathetic with customers.

Philosophy of putting guests first: What the Taj Group looks for in managers is integrity and the ability to work consistently and conscientiously to always put guests first, to respond beyond the call of duty and to work well under pressure. They aren't driven solely by money.

Training Customer Ambassadors: The Taj Group's experience and research have shown that employees make 70% to 80% of their contacts with guests in an unsupervised environment. The employees will usually have to deal with guests without supervision. They were trained what and how to do without supervisor's assistance.

Skill Training: The company imparts the employees' technical skills to master their jobs, grooming, personality and language skills and customer-handling skills, so that they can listen to guests, understand their needs and customize service.

Support of the superiors: Trainees are assured that the company's leadership, right up to the CEO, will support any employee decision to delight the guests.

Decision making freedom: The Taj Group's training programmes not only motivate employees, but they also create a favourable organizational culture. When the Taj Group empowers employees to take decisions as agents of the customer, it energizes them and makes them feel in command. This is a classical example of leadership from below.

Lead by example: The Group expects managers to lead by example. For instance, after a day of work, the general manager of every hotel is expected to be in the lobby in the evenings, to welcome guests. Though old-fashioned it may seem, that's the Taj tradition of hospitality. *(The information is sourced mainly from an article in the internet, "The ordinary Heroes of the Taj" written by Rohit Deshpande and Anjali Raina, Harvard Business Review, December 2011).*

Annexure – 3

BITTEN BY THE BUG OF CONSUMERISM
By Sri. G.G. Menon

Venkat was in his mid-thirties and worked with one of the top IT companies of India at their Bengaluru office. He had been working with the company for more than ten years. His monthly take-home pay was about Rs.95,000. He lived in a rented accommodation with his wife, two sons and his parents. He still had about 25 years of working life left. Of late, he had been toying with the idea of buying a flat in an upscale locality of the city by availing himself of a housing loan from his bank. The motivation came from the fact that many of his colleagues had over the years bought their own flats in that locality while he continued to live in a rented accommodation in a not-so-upscale locality. He consulted his parents, wife and some of his friends. All of them endorsed the idea; after all, he was going to save on the rent and use it to pay part of the EMI and at the end of the repayment period, he would be the owner of a spacious flat in an upscale locality of Bengaluru. One day, he took leave from his office and approached his bank for a loan to buy the flat he had in mind. The bank manager did everything to make things easy for Venkat. The flat was to cost him about Rs.83 lakhs in all. His loan eligibility came to about Rs.63 lakhs. The remaining amount was to come from the financial support his parents were ready to extend. The monthly EMI would come to about Rs.48,000 extending over a repayment period of 25 years. Venkat took the loan and went ahead. Within days, he had vacated his rented accommodation and moved to his new flat.

Everything was hunky-dory for about five years and then, the 2008 meltdown happened. The company where Venkat worked soon found itself in troubled waters as new job orders gradually stopped coming from the U.S. and Europe which were the company's main markets. And then the dreaded pink slips started arriving from the HR Department. Understandably, the earliest targets were the seniors who cost the company more in terms of salaries and perks. It was Venkat's turn one day. The pink slip brought all his plans for the future crashing down. He knocked at many doors for another job. Ultimately, after nine months of unemployment, he landed a job in a small IT firm. But, the salary was not even half of what he was receiving earlier. Paying the EMI for the flat became impossible for Venkat. The bank kept on sending reminders to him for clearing the amount in arrears. But, Venkat was helpless. The bank in exercise of their right of foreclosure moved a court for attaching the flat. The court soon issued the necessary orders. Venkat and his family vacated their dream home, tears welling up in their eyes and shifted to a rented two-room flat in a locality populated mostly by lower middle-class families.

The above story, in many ways, is typical of the havoc that excessive materialism and consumerism is wreaking on the lives of countless number of Indians today. Venkat did not have more than a few thousands of rupees as savings. He had not even insured his life. After paying the EMI of about Rs.48,000/-, he would have with him only about Rs.47,000/- with which he would have to meet all the expenses of his family consisting of himself, his wife, their two school-going kids and his parents who stayed with him. He was clearly overstretching his budget. Perhaps, just one emergency, medical or otherwise, was enough to throw his life out of gear since he hardly had any savings to fall back upon. But, in his all-consuming desire to buy the flat, he had no time to think of such things. Thus, it was that Venkat found himself almost penniless within a few months of getting the pink slip. While the pink slip was the main reason for the upheaval in Venkat's life, was he himself blameless? And what about the bank? Should not they have made a holistic assessment of his finances and suitably advised him against the misadventure? Here was a man who hardly had any savings of his own, not even an insurance policy on his life even though he was holding a highly-paid job. Yet, bitten by the bug of consumerism, he was staking a major part of his future earnings and his parents' savings on buying a flat in an upscale locality. The bank could have asked him to defer his plans till he had built up adequate savings for a rainy day or may be, they could have persuaded him to settle for a house which could be bought with a smaller budget. The bank did nothing of the sort. Was this mechanical 'business-only' approach of the bank correct?

Author's comments: As with most other things, there is an ethical side to banking too. But, the bank in question did not seem to consider this important. That surely is not something a customer expects from his bank. It should be remembered that concern for the overall well-being of a customer is an important part of customer service without which no organization can hope to gain credibility in the public eye.

Annexure - 4

TWO PEARLS OF WISDOM FROM THE ANIMAL KINGDOM

It is a sad fact of life that we cannot communicate with the fauna around us. Had there been a lingua franca for human beings to converse with animals and vice versa, life on this planet could have been much more beautiful and richer. But, even without a lingua franca, there is so much that the animals teach us on a daily basis. What we need to understand these lessons are keen eyes and ears and a receptive mind. Read on....

GEESE FLY IN THE 'V' FORMATION, TEAMWORK PAYS

Geese are a fascinating species of birds. They have been with us since times immemorial with their incredible and unique behavioural dynamics. Every morning and evening, it is common to see these birds flying high in the sky in one direction in a 'V' formation. They flap their wings uniformly in perfect harmony and rhythm. This incredible scene suggests that intelligent planning and thinking are obviously needed to execute this group dynamics on the part of the birds. This is where the role of the leader and other seniors in the group comes in. Let's see why these birds choose the 'V' formation and the advantages it offers.

1. *Geese fly together*

Flying in the 'V' formation, no doubt, spares the birds from the odious routine of constantly watching the back of the bird in front of them. But, the most important advantage of adopting the 'V' formation is that each bird, in a 'V' formation, while flapping its wings creates updrafts i.e. upward movements of air, the benefit of which accrues to each member of the group. As a result, flying becomes easier for the birds and they can fly about 71 times farther than when they are flying alone. Thus the 'formation' helps the birds to achieve their goal much more quickly and much more easily. So much so that when one of the birds falls out of formation, it soon realizes that it takes much more energy to fly alone than as part of a formation. It then moves back into formation and becomes a part of the team again.

This has a lesson for us human beings too, which is that good teamwork enables better efficiency and quicker achievement of goals.

2.T*aking turns to lead*:
As the bird in the lead position does not get the benefit of updrafts, it has to put in more effort than others which can tire out even the strongest lead goose. Due to this, the birds take turns in the lead position: when the lead bird gets tired, it rotates to the back and another bird takes its position. This ensures that none of the birds is overworked while maintaining a consistent efficiency level for the team as a whole.

The lesson for us human beings here is that every member of a team should know and understand leadership lessons and be prepared to take on the responsibility of both leader and supporter from time to time. This ensures that no single member gets overworked and everyone's skills, talents and knowledge are optimally utilized.

3. *Honking to encourage those who are ahead:*
The birds engage in honking to encourage those in front to keep up their pace.

In any team of human beings too, encouraging each other and celebrating the work of an individual member or the team as a whole from time to time is important as such actions build up team spirit and camaraderie among the team members.

4. *They take care of those who are sick:*
If a bird becomes sick, two other birds fall out of the formation to stay with the sick bird. They stay with it until it is able to fly again. Thereafter, they fly back together to catch up with the rest of their group.

For human teams, there is an important lesson here. To build a good and strong team, it is necessary that those who are lagging behind for some reason, personal or otherwise, are well taken care of and duly supported in their bid to bounce back.

Being done with the lesson from the geese, let us now turn to what the spider has to teach us.

"TRY AND TRY AGAIN, TILL YOU SUCCEED "

We have all heard the story of the Scottish King, Robert the Bruce who secured freedom for Scotland by defeating the English forces in the year 1328. But, this victory did not come easy. The King's forces were defeated many times by the enemy. He went into hiding and became a dejected man, broken in spirit. One day, while sitting inside a cave, the King saw a spider trying to weave a web over the ceiling. The spider tried many times. Each time, the thread would break and the spider would fall to the ground. But, it did not give up. Finally, in its tenth attempt, the spider was able to weave a perfect web.

The King was watching the struggles of the spider all the while. When the spider finally succeeded, it sparked a sudden thought process in the King's mind and he instinctively started wondering- "If a spider can win even after so many failures, why can't I?" The King shed his despondency and returned to the battlefield to rally his troops to fight for the independence of their dear Scotland once again. Finally, in 1328, he realized his aim. The lesson the spider taught the King through its struggles was *"Try and try again, till you succeed"* The King did not miss the significance of the spider's actions and acted accordingly. *The same lesson holds for anyone in a leadership position. He must never give up and go on trying till he and his team succeed.* We must remember that in order to inspire followers, a leader needs to be inspirational and to be inspirational a never-say-die spirit and resilience are essential in a leader.

By The Same Author

Uncover insightful 'Life Lessons' through the narrative of this book and get to know the immense hidden potential within you. Embrace the keys to a fulfilling existence by learning to solve your problems of daily living logically, rationally and smoothly. Academic lessons may fade from your memory. These are the lessons, no school or college has taught you. Come rain or shine, internalize the timeless wisdom from the 'Life lessons', it will remain as your enduring guide through life and turn it into a masterpiece.

www.ingramcontent.com/pod-product-compliance
Lightning Source LLC
LaVergne TN
LVHW050546160826
845677LV00011B/2193

* 9 7 9 8 8 9 3 2 2 2 2 0 3 *